KRISHNAMURTI
on
EDUCATION

KRISHNAMURTI

on

EDUCATION

1817

HARPER & ROW, PUBLISHERS
New York, Hagerstown,
San Francisco, London

FIRST EDITION

Designed by Eve Callahan

Library of Congress Cataloging in Publication Data

Krishnamurti, Jiddu, 1895–
   Krishnamurti on education.
   "This book is the outcome of talks and discussions held in India by J. Krishnamurti with the students and teachers of schools at Rishi Valley School in Andhra Pradesh and Rajghat School at Varanasi."
   1. Krishnamurti, Jiddu, 1895– 2. Education—Philosophy. 3. Education—India. I. Title.
LB880.K7414 1977   370.1'092'4   76–62933
ISBN 0-06-064794-9

---

77 78 79 80 81 10 9 8 7 6 5 4 3 2 1

Contents

Foreword

This book is the outcome of talks and discussions held in India by J. Krishnamurti with the students and teachers of schools at Rishi Valley School in Andhra Pradesh and Rajghat School at Varanasi. These centers are run by the Krishnamurti Foundation India, which was set up to create a milieu where the teachings of Krishnamurti could be communicated to the child. Krishnamurti regards education as of prime significance in the communication of that which is central to the transformation of the human mind and the creation of a new culture. Such a fundamental transformation takes place when the child, while being trained in various skills and disciplines, is also given the capacity to be awake to the processes of his own thinking, feeling and action. This alertness makes him self-critical and observant and thus establishes an integrity of perception, discrimination and action, crucial to the maturing within him of a right relationship to man, to nature and to the tools man creates.

There is a questioning today of the basic postulates of the educational structure and its various systems in India and in the rest of the world. At all levels there is a growing realisation that the existing models have failed and that there is a total lack of relevance between the human being and the complex, contemporary society. The ecological crisis and increasing poverty, hunger and violence, are forcing man inevitably to face the realities of the human situation. At a time like this, a completely new approach to the postulates of education is necessary. Krishnamurti questions the roots of our culture. His challenge is addressed not only to the structure of education but to the nature and quality of man's mind and life. Unlike all other attempts to salvage or suggest alternatives to the educational system, Krishnamurti's approach breaks through frontiers of particular cultures and establishes an entirely new set of values, which in turn can create a new civilization and a new society.

To Krishnamurti a new mind is only possible when the religious spirit and the scientific attitude form part of the same movement of consciousness—a state where the scientific attitude and the religious spirit are not two parallel processes or capacities of the mind. They do not exist in watertight compartments as two separate movements that have to be fused but are a new movement inherent in intelligence and in the creative mind.

Krishnamurti talks of two instruments available to the human being—the instrument of knowledge which enables him to gain mastery over technical skills, and intelligence which is born of observation and selfknowing.

While Krishnamurti gives emphasis to the cultivation of the intellect, the necessity to have a sharp, clear, analytical and precise mind, he lays far greater stress on a heightened critical awareness of the inner and outer world, a refusal to accept authority at any level and a harmonious balance of intellect and sensitivity. To discover the areas where knowledge and technical skills are necessary and where they are irrelevant and even harmful, is to Krishnamurti one of the fundamental tasks of education, because it is only when the mind learns the significance of the existence of areas where knowledge is irrelevant that a totally new dimension is realised, new energies generated and the unused potentialities of the human mind activated.

One of the unsolved problems and challenges to educationists all over the world is the problem of freedom and order. How is a child, a student, to grow in freedom and at the same time develop a deep sense of inner order. Order is the very root of freedom. Freedom, to Krishnamurti, has no terminal point but is renewed from moment to moment in the very act of living. In these pages, one can get a glimpse, a feel, of this quality of freedom of which order is an inherent part.

The years which a student spends in a school must leave behind him a fragrance and delight. This can only happen when there is no competition, no authority, when teaching and learning is a simultaneous process in the present, where the educator and the educated are both participating in the act of learning.

Unlike the communication of the religious spirit by various sects and religious groups, Krishnamurti's approach is in a sense truly secular and yet has a deeply religious dimension. There is a departure in Krishnamurti's teachings from the traditional approach of the relationship between the teacher and the taught, the guru and the shishya. The traditional approach is basically hierarchical; there is the teacher who knows and the student who does not know and has to be taught. To Krishnamurti, the teacher and the student function at the same level—communicating through questioning and counter-questioning till the depths of the problem are exposed and understanding is revealed, illuminating the mind of both.

The Krishnamurti Foundation India feels deeply privileged for being able to offer this book to the student and the educator.

—The Editors

TALKS TO
STUDENTS

1 / On Education

You know, you live in one of the most beautiful valleys I have seen. It has a special atmosphere. Have you noticed, especially in the evenings and very early mornings, a quality of silence which permeates, which penetrates the valley? There are around here, I believe, the most ancient hills in the world and man has not spoilt them yet; and wherever you go, in cities or in other places, man is destroying nature, cutting down trees to build more houses, polluting the air with cars and industry. Man is destroying animals; there are very few tigers left. Man is destroying everything because more and more people are born and they must have more space. Gradually, man is spreading destruction all over the world. And when one comes to a valley like this—where there are very few people, where nature is still not spoilt, where there is still silence, quietness, beauty—one is really astonished. Every time one comes here one feels the strangeness of this land, but probably you have become used to it. You do not look at the hills any more, you do not listen to the birds any more and to the wind among the leaves. So you have gradually become indifferent.

Education is not only learning from books, memorising some facts, but also learning how to look, how to listen to what the books are saying, whether they are saying something true or false. All that is part of education. Education is not just to pass examinations, take a degree and a job, get married and settle down, but also to be able to listen to the birds, to see the sky, to see the extraordinary beauty of a tree, and the shape of the hills, and to feel with them, to be really, directly in touch with them. As you grow older, that sense of listening, seeing, unfortunately disappears because you have worries, you want more money, a better car, more children or less children. You become jealous, ambitious, greedy, envious; so you lose the sense of the beauty of the earth. You know what is happening in the world. You must be studying current events. There are wars, revolts, nation divided against nation. In this country too there is division, separation, more and more people being born, poverty, squalor and complete callousness. Man does not care what happens to another so long as he is perfectly safe. And you are being educated to fit into all this. Do you know the world is mad, that all this is madness —this fighting, quarrelling, bullying, tearing at each other? And you will grow up to fit into this. Is this right, is this what education is meant for, that you should willingly or unwillingly fit into this mad structure called society? And do you know what is happening to religions throughout the world? Here also man is disintegrating, nobody believes in anything any more. Man has no faith and religions are merely the result of a vast propaganda.

Since you are young, fresh, innocent, can you look at all the beauty of the earth, have the quality of affection? And can you retain that? For if you do not, as you grow up, you will conform, because that is the easiest way to live. As you grow up, a few of you will revolt, but that revolt too will not answer the problem. Some of you will try to run away from society, but that running away will have no meaning. You have to change society, but not by killing people. Society is you and I. You and I create the society in which we live. So you have to change. You cannot fit into this monstrous society. So what are you going to do?

And you, living in this extraordinary valley, are you going to be thrown into this world of strife, confusion, war, hatred? Are you going to conform, fit in, accept all the old values? You know what these values are—money, position, prestige, power. That is all man wants and society wants you to fit into that pattern of values. But if you now begin to think, to observe, to learn, not from books, but learn for yourself by watching, listening to everything that is happening around you, you will grow up to be a different human being—one who cares, who has affection, who loves people. Perhaps if you live that way, you might find a truly religious life.

So look at nature, at the tamarind tree, the mango trees in bloom, and listen to the birds early in the morning and late in the evening. See the clear sky, the stars, how marvellously the sun sets behind those hills. See all the colours, the light on the leaves, the beauty of the land, the rich earth. Then having seen that and seen also what the world is, with all its brutality, violence, ugliness, what are you going to do?

Do you know what it means to attend, to pay attention? When you pay attention, you see things much more clearly. You hear the bird singing much more distinctly. You differentiate between various sounds. When you look at a tree with a great deal of attention, you see the whole beauty of the tree. You see the leaves, the branch, you see the wind playing with it. When you pay attention, you see extraordinarily clearly. Have you ever done it? Attention is something different from concentration. When you concentrate, you don't see everything. But when you are paying attention, you see a great deal. Now, pay attention. Look at that tree and see the shadows, the slight breeze among the leaves. See the shape of the tree. See the proportion of the tree in relation to other trees. See the quality of light that penetrates through the leaves, the light on the branches and the trunk. See the totality of the tree. Look at it that way, because I am going to talk about something to which you have to pay attention. Attention is very important, in the class, as well as when you are outside, when you are eating, when you are walking. Attention is an extraordinary thing.

I am going to ask you something. Why are you being educated? Do you understand my question? Your parents send you to school. You attend classes, you learn mathematics, you learn geography, you learn history. Why? Have you ever asked why you want to be educated, what is the point of being educated? What is the point of your passing examinations and getting degrees? Is it to get married, get a job and settle down in life as millions and millions of people do? Is that what you are going to do, is that the meaning of education? Do you understand what I am talking about? This is really a very serious question. The whole world is questioning the basis of education. We see what education has been used for. Human beings throughout the world—whether in Russia or in China or in America or in Europe or in this country—are being educated to conform, to fit into society and into their culture, to fit into the stream of social and economic activity, to be sucked into that vast stream that has been flowing for thousands of years. Is that education, or is education something entirely different? Can education see to it that the human mind is not drawn into that vast stream and so destroyed; see that the mind is never sucked into that stream; so that, with such a mind, you can be an entirely different human being with a different quality to life? Are you going to be educated that way? Or are you going to allow your parents, society, to dictate to you so that you become part of the stream of society? Real education means that a human mind, your mind, not only is capable of being excellent in mathematics, geography and history, but also can never, under any circumstances, be drawn into the stream of society. Because that stream which we call living, is very corrupt, is immoral, is violent, is greedy. That stream is our culture. So, the question is how to bring about the right kind of education so that the mind can withstand all temptations, all influences, the bestiality of this civilisation and this culture. We have come to a point in history where we have to create a new culture, a totally different kind of existence, not based on consumerism and industrialisation, but a culture based upon a real quality of religion. Now how does one bring about, through education, a mind that is entirely different, a mind that is not greedy, not envious? How does one create a mind that is not ambitious, that is extraordinarily active, efficient; that has a real perception of what is true in daily life which is after all religion.

Now, let us find out what is the real meaning and intention of education. Can your mind, which has been conditioned by society, the culture in which you have lived, be transformed through education so that you will never under any circumstances enter the stream of society? Is it possible to educate you differently? 'Educate' in the real sense of that word; not to transmit from the teachers to the students some information about mathematics or history or geography, but in the very instruction of these subjects to bring about a change in your mind. Which means that you have to be extraordinarily critical. You have to learn never to accept anything which you yourself do not see clearly, never to repeat what another has said.

I think you should put these questions to yourself, not occasionally, but every day. Find out. Listen to everything, to the birds, to that cow calling. Learn about everything in yourself, because if you learn from yourself about yourself, then you will not be a second-hand human being. So you should, if I may suggest, from now on, find out how to live entirely differently and that is going to be difficult, for I am afraid most of us like to find an easy way of living. We like to repeat and follow what other people say, what other people do, because it is the easiest way to live—to conform to the old pattern or to a new pattern. We have to find out what it means never to conform and what it means to live without fear. This is your life, and nobody is going to teach you, no book, no guru. You have to earn from yourself, not from books. There is a great deal to learn about yourself. It is an endless thing, it is a fascinating thing, and when you learn about yourself from yourself, out of that learning wisdom comes. Then you can live a most extraordinary, happy, beautiful life. Right? Now, will you ask me questions?

Student: The world is full of callous people, indifferent people, cruel people, and how can you change those people?

Krishnamurti: The world is full of callous people, indifferent people, cruel people, and how can you change those people? Is that it? Why do you bother about changing others? Change yourself. Otherwise as you grow up you will also become callous. You will also become indifferent. You will also become cruel. The past generation is vanishing, it is going, and you are coming, and if you also prove callous, indifferent, cruel, you will also build the same society. What matters is that *you* change, that you are not callous, that you are not indifferent. When you say all this is the business of the older generation, have you seen them, have you watched them, have you felt for them? If you have, you will do something. Change yourself and test it by action. Such action is one of the most extraordinary things. But we want to change everybody except ourselves, which means, really, we do not want to change, we want others to change, and so we remain callous, indifferent, cruel, hoping the environment will change so that we can continue in our own way. You understand what I am talking about?

Student: You ask us to change, what do we change into?

Krishnamurti: You ask us to change, what is it we change into? You cannot change into a monkey, probably you would like to, but you cannot. Now when you say, "I want to change into something"—listen to this carefully—if you say to yourself, "I must change, I must change myself into something", the "into something" is a pattern which you have created, haven't you? Do you see that? Look, you are violent or greedy and you want to change yourself into a person who is not greedy. Not wanting to be greedy is another form of greed, isn't it? Do you see that? But if you say, "I am greedy, I will find out what it means, why I am greedy, what is involved in it", then, when you understand greed, you will be free of greed. Do you understand what I am talking about?

Let me explain. I am greedy and I struggle, fight, make tremendous efforts not to be greedy. I have already an idea, a picture, an image of what it means not to be greedy. So I am conforming to an idea which I think is non-greed. You understand? Whereas if I look at my greed, if I understand why I am greedy, the nature of my greed, the structure of greed, then, when I begin to understand all that, I am free of greed. Therefore, freedom from greed is something entirely different from trying to become non-greedy. Do you see the difference? Freedom from greed is something which is entirely different from saying, "I must be a great man so I must be non-greedy?" Have you understood?

I was thinking last night, that I have been to this valley, off and on, for about forty years. People have come and gone. Trees have died and new trees have grown. Different children have come, passed through his school, have become engineers, housewives and disappeared altogether into the masses. I meet them occasionally, at an airport or at a meeting, very ordinary people. And if you are not very careful, you are also going to end up that way.

Student: What do you mean by ordinary?

Krishnamurti: To be like the rest of men; with their worries, with their corruption, violence, brutality, indifference, callousness. To want a job, to want to hold on to a job, whether you are efficient or not, to die in the job. That is what is called ordinary—to have nothing new, nothing fresh, no joy in life, never to be curious, intense, passionate, never to find out, but merely to conform. That is what I mean by ordinary. It is called being bourgeois. It is a mechanical way of living, a routine, a boredom.

Student: How can we get rid of being ordinary?

Krishnamurti: How can you get rid of being ordinary? Do not be ordinary. You cannot get rid of it. Just do not be it.

Student: How, Sir?

Krishnamurti: There is no "how". You see that is one of the most destructive questions: "Tell me how"? Man has always been saying, throughout the world, "Tell me how". If you see a snake, a poisonous cobra, you do not say, "Please tell me how to run away from it". You run away from it. So in the same way, if you see that you are ordinary, run, leave it, not tomorrow, but instantly.

Since you will not ask any more questions. I am going to propose something. You know people talk a great deal about meditation, don't they?

Student: They do.

Krishnamurti: You know nothing about it. I am glad. Because you know nothing about it, you can learn about it. It is like not knowing French or Latin or Italian. Because you do not know, you can learn, you can learn as though for the first time. Those people who already know what meditation is, they have to unlearn and then learn. You see the difference? Since you do not know what meditation is, let us learn about it. To learn about meditation, you have to see how your mind is working. You have to watch, as you watch a lizard going by, walking across the wall. You see all its four feet, how it sticks to the wall, and as you watch, you see all the movements. In the same way, watch your thinking. Do not correct it. Do not suppress it. Do not say, "All this is too difficult". Just watch; now, this morning.

First of all sit absolutely still. Sit comfortably, cross your legs, sit absolutely still, close your eyes, and see if you can keep your eyes from moving. You understand? Your eye balls are apt to move, keep them completely quiet, for fun. Then, as you sit very quietly, find out what your thought is doing. Watch it as you watched the lizard. Watch thought, the way it runs, one thought after another. So you begin to learn, to observe.

Are you watching your thoughts-how one thought pursues another thought, thought saying, "This is a good thought, this is a bad thought"? When you go to bed at night, and when you walk, watch your thought. Just watch thought, do not correct it, and then you will learn the beginning of meditation. Now sit very quietly. Shut your eyes and see that the eye-balls do not move at all. Then watch your thoughts so that you learn. Once you begin to learn there is no end to learning.

2 / On the Religious Mind and the Scientific Mind

Early this morning I saw a beautiful bird, a black bird with a red neck. I do not know what the bird is called. It was flying from tree to tree and there was a song in its heart, and it was a lovely thing to behold. I would like this morning to talk to you of a rather serious matter. You should listen carefully and if you want to, perhaps later on, you may be able to discuss it with your teachers. I want to talk about something which concerns the whole world, about which the whole world is disturbed. It is the question of the religious spirit and the scientific mind. There are these two attitudes in the world. These are the only two states of mind that are of value, the true religious spirit and the true scientific mind. Every other activity is destructive, leading to a great deal of misery, confusion and sorrow.

The scientific mind is very factual. Discovery is its mission, its perception. It sees things through a microscope, through a telescope; everything is to be seen actually as it is; from that perception, science draws conclusions, builds up theories. Such a mind moves from fact to fact. The spirit of science has nothing to do with individual conditions, with nationalism, with race, with prejudice. Scientists are there to explore matter, to investigate the structure of the earth and of the stars and the planets, to find out how to cure man's diseases, how to prolong man's life, to explain time, both the past and the future. But the scientific mind and its discoveries are used and exploited by the nationalistic mind, by the mind that is India, by the mind that is Russia, by the mind that is America. Scientific discovery is utilised and exploited by sovereign states and continents.

Then there is the religious mind, the true religious mind that does not belong to any cult, to any group, to any religion, to any organised church. The religious mind is not the Hindu mind, the Christian mind, the Buddhist mind, or the Muslim mind. The religious mind does not belong to any group which calls itself religious. The religious mind is not the mind that goes to churches, temples, mosques. Nor is it a religious mind that holds to certain forms of beliefs, dogmas. The religious mind is completely alone. It is a mind that has seen through the falsity of churches, dogmas, beliefs, traditions. Not being nationalistic, not being conditioned by its environment, such a mind has no horizons, no limits. It is explosive, new, young, fresh, innocent. The innocent mind, the young mind, the mind that is extraordinarily pliable, subtle, has no anchor. It is only such a mind that can experience that which you call god, that which is not measurable.

A human being is a true human being when the scientific

spirit and the true religious spirit go together. Then human beings will create a good world—not the world of the communist or the capitalist, of Brahmins, or of Roman Catholics. In fact the true Brahmin is the person who does not belong to any religious creed, has no class, no authority; no position in society. He is the true Brahmin, the new human being, who combines both the scientific and the religious mind, and therefore is harmonious without any contradiction within himself. And I think the purpose of education is to create this new mind, which is explosive, and does not conform to a pattern which society has set.

A religious mind is a creative mind. It has not only to finish with the past but also to explode in the present. And this mind —not the interpreting mind of books, of the Gita, the Upanishads, the Bible—which is capable of investigating, is also capable of creating an explosive reality. There is no interpretation here nor dogma.

It is extraordinarily difficult to be religious and to have a clear and precise, scientific mind, to have a mind that is not afraid, that is unconcerned with its own security, its own fears. You cannot have a religious mind without knowing yourself, without knowing all about yourself—your body, your mind, your emotions, how the mind works, how thought functions. And to go beyond all that, to uncover all that, you must approach it with a scientific mind which is precise, clear, unprejudiced, which does not condemn, which observes, which sees. When you have such a mind you are really a cultured human being, a human being who knows compassion. Such a human being knows what it is to be alive.

How does one bring this about? For it is imperative to help the student to be scientific, to think very clearly, precisely, to be sharp, as well as to help him uncover the depths of his mind, to go beyond words, his various labels as the Hindu, Muslim, Christian. Is it possible to educate the student to go beyond all labels and find out, experience that something which is not measured by the mind, which no books contain, to which no guru can lead you? If such an education is possible in a school like this, it will be remarkable. You must all see that it is worthwhile to create such a school. That is what the teachers and I have been discussing for some days. We have talked of a great many things — about authority, about discipline, how to teach, what to teach, what listening is, what education is, what culture is, how to sit still. Merely to pay attention to dance, to song, to arithmetic, to lessons, is not the whole of life. It is also part of life to sit still and look at yourself, to have insight, *to see.* It is also necessary to observe how to think, what to think and why you are thinking. It is also part of life to look at birds, to watch the village people, their squalor — which each one of us has brought about, which society maintains. All this is part of education.

3 / On Knowledge and Intelligence

You are here to gather knowledge—historical, biological, linguistic, mathematical, scientific, geographical, and so on. Apart from the knowledge that you acquire here, there is collective knowledge, the knowledge of the race, of your grandfathers, of your past generations. They all had a great many experiences, a great many things happened to them, and their collective experience has become knowledge. Then there is the knowledge of your own personal experiences, your own reactions, impressions, your own tendencies and inclinations, which have assumed their own peculiar forms. So there is scientific, biological, mathematical, physical, geographical, historical knowledge; there is also the collective knowledge of the past which is the tradition of the community, the race; then there is the personal knowledge which you yourself have experienced. There are these three kinds of knowledge—scientific, collective, personal. Do they collectively make for intelligence?

Now what is knowledge? Is knowledge related to intelligence? Intelligence uses knowledge, intelligence being the capacity to think clearly, objectively, sanely, healthily. Intelligence is a state in which there is no personal emotion involved, no personal opinion, prejudice or inclination. Intelligence is the capacity for direct understanding. I am afraid this is rather difficult, but it is important, it is good for you to exercise your brain. So there is knowledge, which is the past continually being added to, and there is intelligence. Intelligence is the quality of the mind that is very sensitive, very alert, very aware. Intelligence does not hold on to any particular judgement or evaluation, but is capable of thinking very clearly, objectively. Intelligence has no involvement. Are you following? Now, how is this intelligence to be cultivated? What is the capacity of this intelligence? You are living here, being educated in all the various disciplines, in various branches of knowledge. Are you also being educated so that intelligence comes into being at the same time? Do you see the point? You may have a very good knowledge of mathematics or engineering. You may take a degree, enter a college and be a first class engineer. But at the same time, are you becoming sensitive, alert? Are you thinking objectively, clearly, with intelligence, understanding? Is there a harmony between knowledge and intelligence, a balance between the two? You cannot think clearly if you are prejudiced, if you have opinions. You cannot think clearly if you are not sensitive; sensitive to nature, sensitive to all the things that are happening around you, sensitive not only to what is happening outside you but also inside you. If you are not sensitive, if you are not aware, you cannot think clearly. Intelligence implies that you see the beauty of the earth, the beauty of the trees, the beauty of the skies, the lovely sunset, the stars, the beauty of subtlety.

Now, is this intelligence being gathered by you here in this school? Are you gathering it or only gathering knowledge through books? If you have no intelligence, no sensitivity, then knowledge can become very dangerous. It can be used for destructive purposes. This is what the whole world is doing. Have you the intelligence that questions, tries to find out? What are the teachers and you doing to bring about this quality of intelligence, which sees the beauty of the land, the dirt, the squalor, and is also aware of the inner happenings, how one thinks, how one observes the subtlety of thought? Are you doing all this? If not, what is the point of your being educated?

Now what is the function of an educator? Is it merely to give you information, knowledge, or is it to bring about this intelligence in you? If I were a teacher here, do you know what I would do? First of all, I would want you to question me about everything—not about knowledge, that is very simple, but to question me about how to look, how to look at these hills, to look at that tamarind tree, how to listen to a bird, how to follow a stream. I would help you to look at the marvellous earth and nature, the beauty of the land, the redness of the soil. Then I would say, look at the peasants, the villagers. Look at them, do not criticize, just look at their squalor, their poverty, not the way you look at them at present, with utter indifference. There are those huts there, have you been there? Have the teachers been down there and looked at those huts, and if they all have, what have they done? So I will make you look, which is to make you sensitive, and you cannot be sensitive if you are careless, indifferent to everything that is happening around you. Then I would say, "To be intelligent, you must know what you are doing, the way you walk, the way you talk, the way you eat." You understand? I would talk to you about your food. I would say, "Look, discuss, do not be afraid to ask any questions, find out, learn", and in your classes I would discuss a subject with you, how to read, how to learn, what it means to pay attention. If you say you want to look out of the window, I would say look out of the window, see everything that you want to see out of the window, and after you have seen it, look at your book with equal interest and pleasure. Then I would say, "Through books, through discussions I have helped you to be intelligent; let me help you to find out how to live in this world sanely, healthily, not half asleep." That is the function of a teacher, of an educator, not just to give you a lot of data, knowledge, but to show you the whole expanse of life, the beauty of it, the ugliness of it, the delight, the joy, the fear, the agony. So that when you leave this place, you are a tremendous human being who can use your intelligence in life, not just a thoughtless, destructive, callous human being.

Now you have listened, the teachers, the principal and students, you have all listened. What are you going to do about it? You know, it is as much your responsibility, as students, as it is the responsibility of the teachers. It is the responsibility of the students to demand, to ask, not just to say "I will sit down, teach me". It means that you must be tremendously intelligent, sensitive, alive, unprejudiced. It is also essential for the teacher to see that you are intelligent so that when you leave Rishi Valley you leave with a smile, with glory in your heart, so that you are sensitive, ready to cry, to laugh.

Student: If you are very sensitive, do you not think you are apt to become emotional?

Krishnamurti: What is wrong with being emotional? When I see those poor people living in poverty, I feel very strongly. Is that wrong? There is nothing wrong in feeling emotion when you see the squalor, the dirt, the poverty around you. But you also feel strongly if another says something ugly about you. When this happens what will you do? Because of your emotion will you hit back at him? Or because you are sensitive, emotional, will you be aware of what you are going to do? If there is an interval before your response and you observe, are sensitive to it, then in that interval intelligence comes in. Allow that interval; in it begin to watch. If you are tremendously aware of the problem there is instant action and that instant action is the right action of intelligence.

Student: Why are we conditioned?

Krishnamurti: Why do you think we are conditioned? It is very simple. You have asked the question. Now, exercise your brain. Find out why you are conditioned. You are born in this country, you live in an environment, in a culture, you grow into a young child, and then what takes place? Watch the babies around you. Watch the mothers, the fathers, if they are Hindus or Muslims or communists or capitalists; they say to the child, "Do this, do that". The child sees the grand-mother going to a temple, performing rituals, and the child gradually accepts all that. Or the parents may say "I don't believe in rituals" and the child also accepts that. The simple fact is that the mind, the brain of the child is like putty or clay and on that putty, impressions are made, like the grooves in a record. Everything is registered. So in a child everything is registered consciously or unconsciously, until gradually he becomes a Hindu, Muslim, Catholic or a non-believer. He then makes divisions—as my belief, your belief, my god, your god, my country, your country. You have been conditioned to make tremendous effort; you have to make an effort to study, to pass an examination, you have to make an effort to be good.

So, the question is how is the mind, which is conditioned, to unravel itself, to get out of conditioning? How do you propose to get out of it? Now exercise your intelligence to find out. Do not follow somebody who says, "Do this and you will get unconditioned"; find out how you will uncondition yourself. Come on, answer me, tell me, discuss with me.

Student: Can you tell us how to uncondition ourselves?

Krishnamurti: To fall into the trap of another conditioning, is that it? First of all, do you know that you are conditioned? How do you know? Is it only because somebody has told you that you are conditioned that you know? Do you see the difference? That is, somebody tells you that you are hungry, that is one thing, and to know for yourself that you are hungry is altogether different. These two statements are different, aren't they? In the same way, do you know for yourself with-out somebody telling you that you are conditioned, as a

Hindu, a Muslim? Do you know it for yourself?

Now I will ask you a question and see whether there is a gap before you answer it. Right? Now observe, think very clearly, unemotionally, without any prejudice. My question is, are you aware that you are conditioned without being told? Are you aware? It is not so very difficult.

Do you know what it means to be aware? When there is a pain in the thumb, you are aware there is pain, nobody tells you there is pain. You know it. Now, in the same way do you know that you are conditioned, conditioned into thinking that you are a Hindu, that you believe in this, that you do not believe in that, that you must go to a temple, that you must not go to a temple? Are you aware of it?

Student: Yes.

Krishnamurti: You are? Now that you are aware that you are conditioned, what next?

Student: I will then see whether I want to be unconditioned.

Krishnamurti: You are conditioned and you become aware, then what takes place? Then I ask, what is wrong with being conditioned? Now I am conditioned as a Muslim and you are conditioned as a Hindu, right? What takes place? We may live in the same street, but because of my conditioning, my belief, my dogma, and you with your belief, with your dogma, though we may meet in the same street, we are separate, aren't we? So where there is separation there must be conflict. Where there are political, economic, social, nationalistic divisions, there must be conflict. So conditioning is the factor of division. Therefore, in order to live peacefully in this world, let us be free of conditioning, cease to be Muslim or Hindu. This is the factor of intelligence; becoming aware that one is conditioned, then seeing the effect of that conditioning in the world, the divisions, nationalistic, linguistic and so on, and seeing that where there is division there is conflict. When you see this, when you are aware that you are conditioned, that is the operation of intelligence.

That is enough for the day. Do you want to ask more questions?

Student: How can one be free from prejudice?

Krishnamurti: When you say, "how", what do you mean by that word? How am I to get up from this place? All that I have to do is to get up. I never ask how I am to get up? Use your intelligence. Do not be prejudiced. First be aware that you are prejudiced. Do not be told by others that you are prejudiced. They are prejudiced, so do not bother what other people say about your prejudices. First be aware that you are prejudiced. You see what prejudice does—it divides people. Therefore you see that there must be intelligent action, which is that the mind must be capable of being free from prejudice, not ask "how" which means a system, a method. Find out whether your mind can be free from prejudice. See what is involved in it. Why are you prejudiced? Because part of your conditioning is to be prejudiced, and in prejudice there is a great deal of comfort, a great deal of pleasure. So first become aware, become aware of the beauty of the land, become aware of the trees, the colour, the shades, the depth of light, and the beauty of the moving trees, and watch the birds, be aware of all that is around you; then gradually move in, find out, be aware of yourself, be aware how you react in your relationships with your friends—all that brings intelligence. Is that enough for this morning? Then we will do something else.

First of all sit completely quiet, comfortably, sit very quietly, relax, I will show you. Now, look at the trees, at the hills, the shape of the hills, look at them, look at the quality of their colour, watch them. Do not listen to me. Watch and see those trees, the yellowing trees, the tamarind, and then look at the bougainvillea. Look not with your mind but with your eyes. After having looked at all the colours, the shape of the land, of the hills, the rocks, the shadow, then go from the outside to the inside and close your eyes, close your eyes completely. You have finished looking at the things outside, and now with your eyes closed you can look at what is happening inside. Watch what is happening inside you, do not think, but just watch, do not move your eye-balls, just keep them very, very quiet, because there is nothing to see now, you have seen all the things around you, now you are seeing what is happening inside your mind, and to see what is happening inside your mind, you have to be very quiet inside. And when you do this, do you know what happens to you? You become very sensitive, you become very alert to things outside and inside. Then you find out that the outside is the inside, then you find out that the observer is the observed.

4 / On Freedom and Order

It is a lovely morning, isn't it? Cool, fresh, and there is dew on the grass and the birds are singing. I hope you enjoyed this morning, as much as I did, looking out of the window, at the cloudless blue sky, the clear shadows, and the sparkling air and all the birds, the trees, and the earth shouting with joy. I hope you listened.

I would like, this morning, to talk about something that we all must understand. To understand something, one has to listen, as you would listen to those birds. If you would hear that clear call, the song of the bird, you must listen very closely, very attentively, you must follow each note, follow each movement of the sound, see how deeply it goes and how far it reaches. And if you know how to listen, you learn a great deal; to listen is more important than anything else in life. To know how to listen, you have to be very attentive. If your mind, if your thoughts, if your heart is thinking about other things, feeling other things, you cannot listen to the birds. To listen, you have to give your whole attention. When you are watching a bird and are looking at the feathers, the colours, the beak, the size and the lovely shape of the bird, then you are giving your heart, your mind and body, everything that you have, to watch it. And then you are really part of that bird. You really enjoy it. So, in the same way, this morning, please listen, not that you must agree or disagree with what we are talking about, but just listen.

Have you ever sat on the banks of a river and watched the water go by? You cannot do anything about the water. There is the clear water, the dead leaves, the branches. You see a dead animal go by, and you are watching all that. You see the movement of the water, the clarity of the water, the swift current of the water and the fullness of the water. But you cannot do anything. You watch and you let the water flow by. So in the same way listen to what I want to talk about this morning.

Freedom does not exist without order. The two go together. If you cannot have order, you cannot have freedom. The two are inseparable. If you say: "I will do what I like. I will turn up for my meals when I like; I will come to the class when I like"—you create disorder. You have to take into consideration what other people want. To run things smoothly, you have to come on time. If I had come ten minutes late this morning I would have kept you waiting. So I have to have consideration. I have to think of others. I have to be polite, considerate, be concerned about other people. Out of that consideration, out of that thoughtfulness, out of that watchfulness, both outward and inward, comes order and with that order there comes freedom.

You know, soldiers all over the world are drilled every day, they are told what to do, to walk in line. They obey orders implicitly without thinking. Do you know what that does to man? When you are told what to do, what to think, to obey, to follow, do you know what it does to you? Your mind becomes dull, it loses its initiative, its quickness. This external, outward imposition of discipline makes the mind stupid, it makes you conform, it makes you imitate. But if you discipline yourself by watching, listening, being considerate, being very thoughtful—out of that watchfulness, that listening, that consideration for others, comes order. Where there is order, there is always freedom. If you are shouting, talking, you cannot hear what others have to say. You can only hear clearly when you sit quietly, when you give your attention.

Nor can you have order, if you are not free to watch, if you are not free to listen, if you are not free to be considerate. This problem of freedom and order is one of the most difficult and urgent problems in life. It is a very complex problem. It needs to be thought over much more than mathematics, geography or history. If you are not really free, you can never blossom, you can never be good, there can be no beauty. If the bird is not free, it cannot fly. If the seed is not free to blossom, to push out of the earth, it cannot live. Everything must have freedom, including man. Human beings are frightened of freedom. They do not want freedom. Birds, rivers, trees, all demand freedom and man must demand it too, not in half measures, but completely. Freedom, liberty, the independence to express what one thinks, to do what one wants to do, is one of the most important things in life. To be really free from anger, jealousy, brutality, cruelty; to be really free within oneself, is one of the most difficult and dangerous things.

You cannot have freedom merely for the asking. You cannot say, "I will be free to do what I like." Because there are other people also wanting to be free, also wanting to express what they feel, also wanting to do what they wish. Everybody wants to be free, and yet they want to express themselves—their anger, their brutality, their ambition, their competitiveness and so on. So there is always conflict. I want to do something and you want to do something and so we fight. Freedom is not doing what one wants, because man cannot live by himself. Even the monk, even the sannyasi is not free to do what he wants, because he has to struggle for what he wants, to fight with himself, to argue within himself. And it requires enormous intelligence, sensitivity, understanding to be free. And yet it is absolutely necessary that every human being, whatever his culture, be free. So you see, freedom cannot exist without order.

Student: Do you mean that to be free there should be no discipline?

Krishnamurti: I carefully explained that you cannot have freedom without order and order is discipline. I do not like to use that word "discipline" because it is laden with all kinds of meaning. Discipline means conformity, imitation, obedience; it means to do what you are told; doesn't it? But, if you want to be free—and human beings must be completely free, otherwise they cannot flower, otherwise they cannot be real human beings—you have to find out for yourself what it is to be orderly, what it is to be punctual, kind, generous, unafraid. The discovery of all that is discipline. This brings about order. To find out you have to examine and to examine you must be free. If you are considerate, if you are watching, if you are listening, then, because you are free, you will be punctual, you will come to the class regularly, you will study, you will be so alive that you will want to do things rightly.

Student: You say that freedom is very dangerous to man. Why is it so?

Krishnamurti: Why is freedom dangerous? You know what society is?

Student: It is a big group of people which tells you what to do and what not to do.

Krishnamurti: It is a big group of people which tells you what to do and what not to do. It is also the culture, the customs, the habits of a certain community; the social, moral, ethical, religious structure in which man lives, that is generally called society. Now, if each individual in that society did what he liked, he would be a danger to that society. If you did what you liked here in the school, what would happen? You would be a danger to the rest of the school. Wouldn't you? So people do not generally want others to be free. A man who is really free, not in ideas, but inwardly free from greed, ambition, envy, cruelty, is considered a danger to people, because he is entirely different from the ordinary man. So, society either worships him or kills him or is indifferent to him.

Student: You said that we must have freedom and order but how are we to get it?

Krishnamurti: First of all, you cannot depend on others; you cannot expect somebody to give you freedom and order—whether it is your father, your mother, your husband, your teacher. You have to bring it about in yourself. This is the first thing to realise, that you cannot ask anything from another, except food, clothes and shelter. You cannot possibly ask, or look to anyone, your gurus or your gods. Nobody can give you freedom and order. So, you have to find out how to bring about order in yourself. That is, you have to watch and find out for yourself what it means to bring about virtue in yourself. Do you know what virtue is—to be moral, to be good? Virtue is order. So, you have to find out in yourself how to be good, how to be kind, how to be considerate. And out of that consideration, out of that watching, you bring about order and therefore freedom. You depend on others to tell you what you should do, that you should not look out of the window, that you should be punctual, that you should be kind. But if you were to say: "I will look out of the window when I want to look but when I study I am going to look at the book," you bring order within yourself without being told by others.

Student: What does one gain by being free?

Krishnamurti: Nothing. When you talk about what one gains, you are really thinking in terms of merchandise. Are you not? I will do this and in return for it, please give me something. I am kind to you because it is profitable for me. But that is not kindliness. So as long as we are thinking in terms of gaining something, there is no freedom. If you say, "If I get freedom, I will be able to do this and that," then it is not freedom. So do not think in terms of utility. As long as we are thinking in terms of using, there is no question of freedom at all. Freedom can only exist when there is no motive. You do not love somebody because he gives you food, or clothes or shelter. Then it is not love.

Do you ever walk by yourself? Or do you always go with others? If you go out by yourself sometimes, not too far away because you are very young, then you will get to know yourself, what you think, what you feel, what is virtue, what you want to be. Find out. And you cannot find out about yourself if you are always talking, going about with your friends, with half a dozen people. Sit under a tree quietly by yourself, not with a book. Just look at the stars, the clear sky, the birds, the shape of the leaves. Watch the shadow. Watch the bird across the sky. By being with yourself, sitting quietly under a tree, you begin to understand the workings of your own mind and that is as important as going to class.

5 / On Sensitivity

Some of the teachers of this school were discussing with me, the other day, how important it is to be sensitive, how necessary it is to have a sensitive body and a sensitive mind. A human being who is aware of his environment, as well as aware of every movement of thought and feeling, who is a harmonious whole, is sensitive. How does that sensitivity come about? How can there be a complete development of the body, of the emotions, of the capacity to think deeply and widely, so that the whole being becomes astonishingly alive to everything about it, to every challenge, to every influence? And is that possible, in a world like this, a world where technological knowledge is all important, where making money, being an engineer or an electronic expert is assuming such importance? Is it possible to be sensitive? The politician, the electronics expert become marvellous human machines, but lead very narrow lives. They are sorrowful people having no depth in them. All they know is their little world, the world determined by their own field.

A life that is held in technological knowledge is a very narrow, limited life. It is bound to breed a great deal of sorrow and misery. But can one have technological knowledge, be able to do things, make a little money and still live in the world with intensity, with intensity, with clarity, with vision? That is the real question. Life is not merely going to the office day after day. Life is extraordinarily vital, important, and for that you must be sensitive, you must have the sensitivity that appreciates beauty. You know, there is something extraordinary about beauty. Beauty is never personal, though we make it personal. We put flowers in our hair, have nice saris, wear fine shirts and trousers, look very smart and try to be as beautiful as we can; that is a very limited beauty. I do not say that you should not wear nice clothes, but merely that—that is not appreciation of beauty. The appreciation of beauty is to see a tree, to see a painting, to see a statue, to see the clouds, the skies, the birds on the wing, to see the morning star, and the sunset behind these hills. To see such immense beauty we must cut through our little personal lives.

You may have good taste. Do you know what good taste means? To know how to combine colours, how not to wear colours that jar, not to say something that is cruel about anybody, to feel kindly, to see the beauty of a house, to have good pictures in your room, to have a room with right proportions. All that is good taste, which can be cultivated. But good taste is not the appreciation of beauty. Beauty is never personal.

When beauty is made personal it becomes self-centered. Self concern is the source of sorrow. You know, most people are not happy in the world. They have money, they have position and power. But remove the money, the position, the power and you see underneath an extreme shallowness of heart. The source of their shallowness, misery, conflict and extreme anguish is a feeling of guilt and fear.

To really appreciate beauty is to see a mountain, to see the lovely trees without the "you" being there; to enjoy them, to look at them although they may belong to another; to see the flow of a river and move with it from beginning to end; to be lost in the beauty, in the vitality, in the rapidity of the river. But you cannot do all that if you are merely concerned with power, with money, with a career. That is only a part of life and to be concerned only with a part of life is to be insensitive and, therefore, to lead a life of shallowness and misery. A petty life always produces misery and confusion not only for itself but for others. I am not moralising, I am just stating the facts of existence.

The function of your teachers is to educate not only the partial mind but the totality of the mind; to educate you so that you do not get caught in the little whirlpool of existence but live in the whole river of life. This is the whole function of education. The right kind of education cultivates your whole being, the totality of your mind. It gives your mind and heart a depth, an understanding of beauty.

Probably, the girls among you will grow up and get married and the boys will have careers and that will be the end. You know, the moment you get married—I am not saying you should not get married—you have your husband, children, and responsibilities begin to crowd in like crows upon a tree. The husband, the house, your children, become a habit and you become caught in that habit. All through your life, till you die, you will be working, working in the house or going to the office, every day.

I wondered—the other morning when I saw you all having a good time—what is going to happen to you all? Will you live a life with a fire burning in you or will you become for the rest of your life a businessman or a housewife? What are you going to do? Should you not be educated to cut through respectability, to burst through all conformity? Probably I am saying something dangerous, but it does not matter. Perhaps you will give an ear and perhaps this will sink somewhere into your consciousness and perhaps in a moment when you are about to make a decision, this may alter the course of your life.

Student: How is one to be sensitive?

Krishnamurti: I do not know if you noticed the other evening, it was drizzling. There was a sharp shower. There were dark, heavy, rain-laden clouds. There were also clouds that were full of light, white, with a rose-coloured light inside them. And there were clouds that were almost like feathers going by. It was a marvellous sight and there was great beauty. If you do not see and feel all these things when you are young, when you are still curious, when you are still indecisive, when you are still looking, searching, asking; if you do not feel now, then you never will. As you grow older life encloses you, life becomes hard. You hardly look at the hills, a beautiful face or a smile. Without feeling affection, kindness, tenderness, life becomes very dreary, ugly, brutal. And as you grow older, you fill your lives with politics, with concern over your jobs, over your families. You become afraid and gradually lose that extraordinary quality of looking at the sunset, at clouds, at the stars of an evening. As you grow older, the intellect begins to create havoc with your lives. I do not mean that you must not have a clear, reasoning intellect, but the predominance of it makes you dull, makes you lose the finer things of life.

You must feel very strongly about everything, not just one or two things, but about everything. If you feel very strongly, then little things will not fill your life. Politics, jobs, careers are all little things. If you feel strongly, if you feel vitally, vigorously, you will live in a state of deep silence. Your mind will be very clear, simple, strong. As men grow older they lose this quality of feeling, this sympathy, this tenderness for others. Having lost it they begin to invent religions. They go to temples, take drinks, drugs, to awaken this spontaneity. They become religious. But religion in the world is put together by man. All temples, churches, dogmas, beliefs are invented by man. Man is afraid because he is lost without a deep sense of beauty, a deep sense of affection. And, having lost this, superficial ceremonies, going to temples, repeating mantras, rituals become very important. In reality, they have no importance at all. Religion born of fear becomes ugly superstition.

So, one has to understand fear. You know, one is afraid: afraid of one's parents, afraid of not passing examinations, afraid of one's teachers, afraid of the dog, afraid of the snake. You have to understand fear and be free of fear. When you are free of fear there is the strong feeling of being good, of thinking very clearly, of looking at stars, of looking at clouds, of looking at faces with a smile. And when there is no fear, you can go much further. Then you can find out for yourself that for which man has searched generation upon generation.

In caves in the south of France and in northern Africa there are 25,000-year-old paintings of animals fighting men, of deer, of cattle. They are extraordinary paintings. They show man's endless search, his battle with life and his search for the extraordinary thing called God. But he never finds that extraordinary thing. You can only come upon it darkly, unknowingly, when there is no fear of any kind. The moment there is no fear you have very strong feelings. The stronger you feel, the less you are concerned about small things. It is fear that drives away all feeling of beauty, of the quality of great silence. As you study mathematics, so you have to study fear. You must know fear and not escape from it so that you can look at fear. It is like going for a walk and suddenly coming upon a snake, jumping away and watching the snake. If you are very quiet, very still, unafraid, then you can look very closely, keeping a safe distance. You can look at the black tongue and the eyes that have no eyelids. You can look at the scales, the patterns of the skin. If you watch the snake very closely you see and appreciate it and perhaps have great affection for that snake. But you cannot look if you are afraid, if you run away. So, in the same way as you look at a snake, you have to look at this battle called life, with its sorrow, misery, confusion, conflict, war, hatred, greed, ambition, anxiety and guilt. You can only look at life and love if there is no fear.

Student: Why do we all want to live?

Krishnamurti: Don't laugh because a little boy asks, when life is so transient, why do we crave to live? Isn't it very sad for a little boy to ask that question? That means he has seen for himself that everything passes away. Birds die, leaves fall, people grow old, man has disease, pain, sorrow, suffering; a little joy, a little pleasure and unending work. And the boy asks why do we cling to all this? He sees how young people grow old before their age, before their time. He sees death. And man clings to life because there is nothing else to cling to. His gods, his temples, don't contain truth; his sacred books are just words. So he asks why people cling to life when there is so much misery. You understand? What do you answer? What do the older people answer? What do the teachers of this school answer? There is silence. The older people have lived on ideas, on words and the boy says, "I am hungry, feed me with food, not with words." He does not trust you and so he asks, "Why do we cling to all this?" Do you know why you cling? Because you know nothing else. You cling to your house, you cling to your books, you cling to your idols, gods, conclusions, your attachments, your sorrows, because you have nothing else and all that you do brings unhappiness. To find out if there is anything else, you must let go what you cling to. If you want to cross the river, you must move away from this bank. You cannot sit on one bank. You want to be free from misery and yet you will not cross the river. So, you cling to something that you know however miserable it is and you are afraid to let go because you don't know what is on the other side of the river.

6 / On Fear

I am sure you have often heard from politicians, from educators, from your parents and from the public that you are the coming generation. But when they talk about you as a new generation, they really do not mean it because they make sure that you conform to the older pattern of society. They really do not want you to be a new, different kind of human being. They want you to be mechanical, to fit in with tradition, to conform, to believe, to accept authority. In spite of this, if you can actually free yourself from fear, not theoretically, not ideally, not merely outwardly but actually, inwardly, deeply, then you can be a different human being. Then you can become the coming generation. The older people are ridden with fear—fear of death, fear of losing jobs, fear of public opinion. They are completely held in the grip of fear. So their gods, their scriptures, their *pujas* are all within the field of fear and therefore the mind is curiously warped, perverted. Such a mind cannot think straight, cannot reason logically, sanely, healthily, because it is rooted in fear. Watch the older generation and you will see how fearful it is of everything—of death, of disease, of going against the current of tradition, of being different, of being new.

Fear is what prevents the flowering of the mind, the flowering of goodness. Most of us learn through fear. Fear is the essence of authority and obedience; parents and governments demand obedience. There is the authority of the book; the authority according to Sankara, Buddha; the authority according to Einstein. Most people are followers; they make the originator into an authority and through propaganda, through influence, through literature, they imprint on the delicate brain the necessity of obedience. What happens to you when you obey? You cease to think. Because you feel that the authorities know so much, are such powerful people, have so much money, can turn you out of the house, because they use the words "duty, love," you succumb, you yield, you begin to obey, and become a slave to an idea, to an impression, to influence. When the brain is conforming to a pattern of obedience, it is no longer capable of freshness, no longer capable of thinking simply and directly.

Now, is it possible to learn without authority? Do you know what learning is? Acquiring knowledge is one thing but learning is an altogether different thing. A machine can acquire information like a robot or like an electronic computer. A machine acquires knowledge because it is being fed certain information. It gathers more and more information which then becomes knowledge. It has the capacity to acquire information, store it and respond when it is asked a question. On the other hand when the human mind can learn, then it is capable of more than just acquiring and storing up. But there can be learning only when the mind is fresh, when it does not say "I know." So, one must differentiate, separate learning from acquiring knowledge. Acquiring knowledge makes you mechanical but learning makes the mind very fresh, young, subtle. And you cannot learn if you are merely following the authority of knowledge. Most educators, right through the world, are merely acquiring and imparting knowledge and so are making the mind mechanical and incapable of learning. You can only learn when you do not know. Learning only comes into being when there is no fear and when there is no authority.

The question is, how do you teach mathematics, or any other subject without authority, and therefore, without fear? Fear is essentially involved in competition. Whether it is competition in a class or competition in life. To be afraid of being nobody, of not arriving, of not succeeding, is at the root of competition. But when there is fear, you cease to learn. And so it seems to me that it is the function of education to eliminate fear, to see that you do not become mechanical and at the same time to give you knowledge. To learn without becoming mechanical, which means to learn without fear, is a complex issue. It involves the elimination of all competition. In this process of competition, you conform, and gradually you destroy the subtlety, the freshness, the youth of the brain. But you cannot deny knowledge. So, is it possible to have knowledge and yet learn to be free from fear? Do you see this?

When do you learn most? Have you ever watched yourself learning? Try to watch yourself sometimes and observe yourself learning. You learn most when you have no fear, when you are not threatened by authority, when you are not competing with your neighbour. Then your mind becomes extraordinarily alive. So the issue for the teacher and the issue for you, as a student, is to learn without authority, to acquire knowledge without perverting or dulling the brain and to eliminate fear. Do you see the problem? To learn there must be no conformity, no authority and yet you must acquire knowledge. To combine all this without distorting the brain, is the problem. So that when you grow older, when you pass your examinations and marry, you meet life with a freshness, without fear. Then you are learning about life all the time; not merely interpreting life according to your pattern.

Do you know what life is? You are too young to know. I will tell you. Have you seen those villagers in tattered clothes, dirty, perpetually starved, working every day of their lives? That is part of life. Then you see a man riding in a car, his wife covered with jewels, with perfume, having many servants. That is also part of life. Then there is the man who voluntarily gives up riches, lives a very simple life, who is anonymous, does not want to be known, does not proclaim that he is a saint. That is also part of life. Then there is the man who wants to become a hermit, a *sannyasi,* and there is also the man who becomes a devotee, who does not want to think, who just blindly follows. That is also part of life. Then there is the man who carefully, logically, sanely thinks, and finding that such thoughts are limited goes beyond thought. That is also part of life. And death is also a part of life, the loss of everything. Belief in the gods and godesses, in saviours, in paradise, in hell, is a part of life. It is a part of life to love, to hate, to feel jealous, to feel greedy, and it is also part of life to go beyond all these trivial things. It is no good growing up and accepting one part of life, the mechanical part concerned with acquiring knowledge, which is to accept the pattern of values created by the past generation. Your parents happen to have money, they send you to school and then to college, they see that you have a job. Then you get married and that is the end of it. All this is only a small segment of life. But there is this vast field of life, an incredibly vast field, to understand which there must be no fear, and that is very difficult.

One of the more vital issues in life is the fact that one withers away, disintegrates. Fear and deterioration are related. As you grow older, unless you solve the problem of fear as it arises, immediately, without carrying it over to tomorrow, the deteriorating factor sets in. It is like a disease, like a wound which festers, destroys. Fear of not getting a better job, of not fulfilling yourself, eat into your capacity, your sensitivity, your intellectual, moral fibre. So the solving of the problem of fear and the factor of deterioration are related. Try and find out what you are afraid of and see if you cannot go beyond that fear, not verbally, not theoretically, but actually. Do not accept authority. Acceptance of authority is obedience which only breeds further fear.

To understand this extraordinarily complex thing called life, which is both in time and beyond time, you must have a very young, fresh, innocent mind. A mind that carries fear within itself, day after day, month after month, is a mechanical mind. And you see machines cannot solve human problems. You cannot have an innocent fresh young mind if you are ridden with fear, if from childhood until you die, you are trained in fear. That is why a good education, a true education eliminates fear.

Student: How can one be completely free from fear?

Krishnamurti: First of all, you must know what fear is. If you know your wife, husband, parent, society, you are no longer afraid of them. To know about something completely makes the mind free from fear.

How will you find out about fear? Are you afraid of public opinion, public opinion being what your friends think of you? Most of us, especially while we are young, want to look alike, dress alike, talk alike. We do not want to be even slightly different, because to be different implies not to conform, not to accept the pattern. When you begin to question the pattern there is fear. Now examine that fear, go into it. Do not say, "I am afraid", and run away from it. Look at it, face it, find out why you are afraid.

Suppose I am afraid of my neighbour, my wife, my god, my country—now what is that fear? Is it actual or is it merely in thought, in time? I will take a simpler example. We are all going to die some time or other. Death is inevitable for all of us and thinking about death creates fear, thinking about something which I do not know creates fear. But if it were actual, if death were there immediately and I were going to die now, there is no fear. You understand? Thought in time creates fear. But if something has to be done immediately there is no fear, because thinking is not possible. If I am going to die the next instant, then I face it, but give me an hour, and I begin to say, "My property, my children, my country, I have not finished my book." I get nervous, frightened.

So fear is always in time, because time is thought. To eliminate fear you have to consider thought as time and then enquire into this whole process of thinking. It is a little bit difficult.

I am afraid of my parents, my society, of what they will say tomorrow or ten days later. My thinking about what might happen projects fear. So can I say, "I am going to look at that fear now, not ten days later"? Can I invite what they are going to say in the present and look at it and if they happen to be right, can I accept it? Why should I be frightened? And if they are wrong, I also accept that. Why should they not be wrong? Why should I be frightened? And I will listen to the teacher to learn, but I am not going to be frightened. So, when I face fear it goes away. But to face fear, I have to enquire, which is quite a complex process because it involves the problem of time.

You know, there are two kinds of time: time by the watch, the next minute, tonight, the day after tomorrow; and there is another kind of time which is created by the psyche inside one, by thought—"I shall be a great man", "I shall have a job", "I shall go to Europe"—that is the psychological future, in time and space. Now to understand chronological time by the watch and to understand time as thought and to go beyond both, is really to be free of fear.

Student: You said if you know something, you stop feeling afraid of it. But how do you know what death is?

Krishnamurti: That is a good question. You are asking, "How do you know what death is and how can you cease to be frightened of it?" I am going to show you. You know there are two kinds of death—bodily death and death of thought. The body is going to die inevitably—like a pencil writing, it eventually wears out. Doctors may invent new kinds of medicine; you may last one hundred and twenty years instead of eighty years. But still there will be death. The physical organism comes to an end. We are not afraid of that. What we are afraid of is the coming to an end of thought, of the "me" that has lived so many years, the "me" that has acquired so much money, that has a family, children, that wants to become important, that wants to have more property, money. That "me" dying is what I am afraid of. Do you see the difference between the two? The physical dying and the "me" dying?

The "me" dying is psychologically much more important than the body's dying and that is what we are frightened of. Now take one pleasure, and die to it. I will explain this to you. You see I do not want to go into the whole problem; I am merely indicating something. You see the "me" is the collection of many pleasures and many pains. Can that "me" die to one thing? Then it will know what death means. That is, can I die to a wish? Can I say "I do not want that wish, I do not want that pleasure"? Can I end it, die to it? Do you know anything about meditation?

Student: No, Sir.

Krishnamurti: But the older people do not know either.

They sit in a corner, close their eyes and concentrate, like school boys trying to concentrate on a book. That is not meditation. Meditation is something extraordinary, if you know how to do it. I am going to talk a little about it.

First of all, sit very quietly; do not force yourself to sit quietly, but sit or lie down quietly without force of any kind. Do you understand? Then watch your thinking. Watch what you are thinking about. You find you are thinking about your shoes, your saris, what you are going to say, the bird outside to which you listen; follow such thoughts and enquire why each thought arises. Do not try to change your thinking. See why certain thoughts arise in your mind so that you begin to understand the meaning of every thought and every feeling without any enforcement. And when a thought arises, do not condemn it, do not say it is right, it is wrong, it is good, it is bad. Just watch it, so that you begin to have a perception, a consciousness which is active in seeing every kind of thought, every kind of feeling. You will know every hidden secret thought, every hidden motive, every feeling, without distortion, without saying it is right, wrong, good or bad. When you look, when you go into thought very very deeply, your mind becomes extraordinarily subtle, alive. No part of the mind is asleep. The mind is completely awake.

That is merely the foundation. Then your mind is very quiet. Your whole being becomes very still. Then go through that stillness, deeper, further—that whole process is meditation. Meditation is not to sit in a corner repeating a lot of words; or to think of a picture and go into some wild, ecstatic imaginings.

To understand the whole process of your thinking and feeling is to be free from all thought, to be free from all feeling so that your mind, your whole being becomes very quiet. And that is also part of life and with that quietness, you can look at the tree, you can look at people, you can look at the sky and the stars. That is the beauty of life.

7 / On Violence

There is a great deal of violence in the world. There is physical violence and also inward violence. Physical violence is to kill another, to hurt other people consciously, deliberately, or without thought, to say cruel things, full of antagonism and hate; and inwardly, inside the skin, to dislike people, to hate people, to criticise people. Inwardly, we are always quarrelling, battling, not only with others, but with ourselves. We want people to change, we want to force them to our way of thinking.

In the world, as we grow up, we see a great deal of violence, at all levels of human existence. The ultimate violence is war—the killing for ideas, for so called religious principles, for nationalities, the killing to preserve a little piece of land. To do that, man will kill, destroy, maim and also be killed himself. There is enormous violence in the world; the rich wanting to keep people poor and the poor wanting to get rich and in the process hating the rich. And you, being caught in society, are also going to contribute to this.

There is violence between husband, wife and children. There is violence, antagonism, hate, cruelty, ugly criticism, anger—all this is inherent in man, inherent in each human being. It is inherent in you. And education is supposed to help you to go beyond all that, not merely to pass an examination and get a job. You have to be educated so that you become a really beautiful, healthy, sane, rational human being, not a brutal man with a very clever brain who can argue and defend his brutality. You are going to face all this violence as you grow up. You will forget all that you have heard here, and will be caught in the stream of society. You will become like the rest of the cruel, hard, bitter, angry, violent world and you will not help to bring about a new society, a new world.

But a new world is necessary. A new culture is necessary. The old culture is dead, buried, burnt, exploded, vapourised. You have to create a new culture. A new culture cannot be based on violence. The new culture depends on you because the older generation has built a society based on violence, based on aggressiveness and it is this that has caused all the confusion, all the misery. The older generations have produced this world and you have to change it. You cannot just sit back and say, "I will follow the rest of the people and seek success and position." If you do, your children are going to suffer. You may have a good time, but your children are going to pay for it. So, you have to take all that into account, the outward cruelty of man to man in the name of god, in the name of religion, in the name of self-importance, in the name of the security of the family. You will have to consider the outward cruelty and violence, and the inward violence which you do not yet know.

You are still young but as you grow older you will realize how inwardly man goes through hell, goes through great misery, because he is in constant battle with himself, with his wife, with his children, with his neighbours, with his gods. He is in sorrow and confusion and there is no love, no kindliness, no generosity, no charity. And a person may have a Ph.D after his name or he may become a businessman with houses and cars but if he has no love, no affection, kindliness, no consideration, he is really worse than an animal because he contributes to a world that is destructive. So, while you are young, you have to know all these things. You have to be shown all these things. You have to be exposed to all these things so that your mind begins to think. Otherwise you will become like the rest of the world. And without love, without affection, without charity and generosity life becomes a terrible business. That is why one has to look into all these problems of violence. Not to understand violence is to be really ignorant, is to be without intelligence and without culture. Life is something enormous, and merely to carve out a little hole for oneself and remain in that little hole, fighting off everybody, is not to live. It is up to you. From now on you have to know about all these things. You have to choose deliberately to go the way of violence or to stand up against society.

Be free, live happily, joyously, without any antagonism, without any hate. Then life becomes something quite different. Then life has a meaning, is full of joy and clarity.

When you woke up this morning, did you look out of the window? If you did, you would have seen those hills become saffron as the sun rose against that lovely blue sky. And as the birds began to sing and the early morning cuckoo cooed, there was a deep silence all around, a sense of great beauty and loneliness, and if one is not aware of all that, one might just as well be dead. But only a very few people are aware. You can be aware of it only when your mind and heart are open, when you are not frightened, when you are no longer violent. Then there is joy, there is an extraordinary bliss of which very few people know, and it is part of education to bring about that state in the human mind.

Student: Will complete destruction of society bring about a new culture, Sir?

Krishnamurti: Will complete destruction bring about a new culture? You know there have been revolutions—the French Revolution, the Russian Revolution, the Chinese Revolution. They destroyed everything to start anew. Have they produced anything new? Every society has three stages or hierarchies— the high, the middle, the low; the high being the aristocracy, the rich people, the clever people; then the middle class, who are always working, then the labourer. Now each is in battle with the other. The middle wants to get to the top and they bring about a revolution and then when they get to the top, they hold on to their positions, their prestige, their welfare, their fortunes, and again the new middle class tries to come to the top. The low trying to reach the middle, and the middle trying to reach the top; this is the battle going on all the time, throughout society and in all cultures. And the middle says: "I am going to get to the top and revolutionize things", and when it gets to the top, you see what it does. It knows how to control people through thought, through torture, through killing, through destruction, through fear.

So, through destruction you can never produce anything. But if you understand the whole process of disorder and destruction, if you study it, not only outwardly but in yourself, then out of that understanding, care, affection, love, out of that comes a totally different order. But if you do not understand, if you merely revolt, it is the same pattern repeated again and again, because we human beings are always the same. You know, it is not like a house that can be pulled down and a new house built. Human beings are not made that way, because human beings are outwardly educated, cultured, clever, but inwardly, they are violent. Unless that animal instinct is fundamentally changed, whatever the outward circumstances are, the inward always overcomes the outer. Education is the change of the inner man.

Student: Sir, you said you must change the world. How can you change it, sir?

Krishnamurti: What is the world? The world is where you live—your family, your friends, your neighbours. And your family, your friends, your neighbours can be extended and that is the world. Now, you are the centre of that world. That is the world you live in. Now how will you change the world? By changing yourself?

Student: Sir, how can you change yourself?

Krishnamurti: How can you do it? First see it. First see that you are the centre of this world. You with your family, are the centre. That is the world and you have to change and you ask, "How am I to change?" How do you change? That is one of the most difficult things—to change—because most of us do not want to change. When you are young, you want to change. You are full of vitality, full of energy, you want to climb trees, you want to look, you are full of curiosity and as you get a little older, go to college, you already begin to settle down. You do not want to change. You say, "For god's sake, leave me alone." Very few people want to change the world and still fewer want to change themselves, because they are the centre of the world in which they live. And to bring about a change requires tremendous understanding. One can change from this to that. But that is not change at all. When people say, "I am changing from this to that", they think they are moving. They think they are changing. But in actual fact they have not moved at all. What they have done is projected an idea of what they should be. The idea of what they "should be" is different from "what is". And the change towards "what should be" is, they think, a movement. But it is not a movement. They think it is change, but what is change is first to be aware of what actually "is" and to live with it, and then one observes that the "seeing" itself brings about change.

Student: Is there any need for one to be serious?

Krishnamurti: Is there any need for one to be serious? A very good question, sir. First of all, what do you mean by serious? Have you ever thought what it means to be serious? Is it the stopping of laughter? To have a smile on your face, would that indicate that you are not serious? To want to look at a tree and see the beauty of a tree, would that be lack of seriousness? To want to know why people look that way, what they wear, why they talk that way, would that be, lack of seriousness? Or would seriousness be always having a long face, always saying: "Am I doing the right thing, am I conforming to a pattern?" I should say that would not be seriousness at all. Trying to meditate is not seriousness, trying to follow the pattern of society is not seriousness—whether it is the pattern of Buddha or Sankara. Merely to conform is never to be serious. That is mere imitation. So you can be serious with a smile on your face, you can be serious when you look at a tree, you can be serious when you paint a picture, when you are listening to music. The quality of seriousness is to pursue to the very end a thought, an idea, a feeling; to go to the very end of it, not to be dissuaded by any other factor; to enquire into every thought to the very end of it whatever may happen to you, even if you have to starve in that process, lose all your property, everything; to go to the very end of thought is to be serious. Have I answered your question, sir?

Student: Yes sir.

Krishnamurti: I am afraid I have not. You have agreed very easily because you have not really understood what I said. Why do you not stop me and say: "Look, I do not understand what you are talking about." That would be straight, that would be serious. If you do not understand something, it does not matter who says it, even god himself, say, "I do not understand what you are talking about, tell me more clearly;" that would be serious. But to meekly agree because a man says so, that shows lack of seriousness. Seriousness consists in seeing things clearly, in finding out, in not accepting. But later on, when you get married and have children and responsibilities, there is a different kind of seriousness. Then you do not want to break the pattern, you want shelter, you want to live in a safe enclosure, free of all revolutions.

Student: Why is one seeking to have pleasure and discard pain?

Krishnamurti: You are rather serious this morning, aren't you? Why? Because you think pleasure is more convenient, is it not? Sorrow is painful. The one you want to avoid, and the other you want to cling to. Why? It is a natural instinct to avoid pain, is it not? If I have a tooth-ache, I want to avoid it. I want to go for a walk which is pleasurable. The problem is not pleasure and pain, but the avoidance of one or the other. Life is both pleasure and pain, is it not? Life is both darkness and light. On a day like this, there are clouds and there is the sun shining; then there is winter and spring; they are part of life, part of existence. But why should we avoid one and cling to the other? Why should we cling to pleasure and avoid pain? Why not merely live with both? The moment you want to avoid pain, sorrow, you are going to invent escapes, quote the Buddha, the Gita, go to the cinema or invent beliefs. The problem is not resolved by either sorrow or pleasure. So don't cling to pleasure or escape from pain. If you cling to pleasure what happens? You get attached, do you not? And if anything happens to the person to whom you are attached or to your property or to your opinion, you are lost. So you say there must be detachment. Do not be either attached or detached; just look at the facts, and when you understand the facts, then there is neither pleasure nor pain; there is merely the fact.

8 / On Image-Making

When we are very young it is a delight to be alive, to hear the birds of the morning, to see the hills after rain, to see those rocks shining in the sun, the leaves sparkling, to see the clouds go by and to rejoice on a clear morning with a full heart and a clear mind. We lose this feeling when we grow up, with worries, anxieties, quarrels, hatreds, fears and the everlasting struggle to earn a livelihood. We spend our days in battle with each other, disliking and liking, with a little pleasure now and then. We never hear the birds, see the trees as we once saw them, see the dew on the grass and the bird on the wing and the shiny rock on a mountainside glistening in the morning light. We never see all that when we are grown up. Why? I do not know if you have ever asked that question. I think it is necessary to ask it. If you do not ask it now, you will soon be caught. You will go to college, get married, have children, husbands, wives, responsibilities, earn a livelihood, and then you will grow old and die. That is what happens to people. We have to ask now, why we have lost this extraordinary feeling for beauty, when we see flowers, when we hear birds? Why do we lose the sense of the beautiful? I think we lose it primarily because we are so concerned with ourselves. We have an image of ourselves.

Do you know what an image is? It is something carved by the hand, out of stone, out of marble, and this stone carved by the hand is put in a temple and worshipped. But it is still handmade, an image made by man. You also have an image about yourself, not made by the hand but made by the mind, by thought, by experience, by knowledge, by your struggle, by all the conflicts and miseries of your life. As you grow older, that image becomes stronger, larger, all-demanding and insistent. The more you listen, act, have your existence in that image, the less you see beauty, feel joy at something beyond the little promptings of that image.

The reason why you lose this quality of fullness is because you are so self-concerned. Do you know what that phrase "to be self-concerned" means? It is to be occupied with oneself, to be occupied with one's capacities whether they are good or bad, with what your neighbours think of you, whether you have a good job, whether you are going to become an important man, or be thrown aside by society. You are always struggling in the office, at home, in the fields; wherever you are, whatever you do, you are always in conflict, and you do not seem to be able to get out of conflict; not being able to get out of it, you create the image of a perfect state, of heaven, of god —again another image made by the mind. You have images not only inwardly but also deeper down, and they are always in conflict with each other. So the more you are in conflict—and conflict will always exist so long as you have images, opinions, concepts, ideas about yourself—the greater will be the struggle.

So the question is: Is it possible to live in this world without an image about yourself? You function as a doctor, a scientist, a teacher, a physicist. You use that function to create the image about yourself, and so, using function, you create conflict in functioning, in doing. I wonder if you understand this? You know, if you dance well, if you play an instrument, a violin, a veena, you use the instrument or the dance to create the image about yourself to feel how marvellous you are, how wonderfully well you play or dance. You use the dancing, the playing of the instrument, in order to enrich your own image of yourself. And that is how you live, creating, strengthening that image of yourself. So there is more conflict; the mind gets dull and occupied with itself; and it loses the sense of beauty, of joy, of clear thinking.

I think it is part of education to function without creating images. You then function without the battle, the inward struggle that goes on within yourself.

There is no end to education. It is not that you read a book, pass an examination and finish with education. The whole of life, from the moment you are born till the moment you die is a process of learning. Learning has no end and that is the timeless quality of learning. And you cannot learn if you are in battle, if you are in conflict with yourself, with your neighbour, with society. You are always in conflict with society, with your neighbour as long as there is an image. But if you are learning about the mechanics of putting together that image, then you will see that you can look at the sky, then you can look at the river and the raindrops on the leaf, feel the cool air of a morning and the fresh breeze among the leaves. Then life has an extraordinary meaning. Life in itself, not the significance given by the image to life—life itself has an extraordinary meaning.

Student: When you are looking at a flower, what is your relationship with the flower?

Krishnamurti: You look at a flower, and what is your relationship to the flower? Do you look at the flower or do you think you are looking at the flower? You see the difference? Are you actually looking at the flower or you think you ought to look at the flower or are you looking at the flower with an image you have about the flower—the image being that it is a rose? The word is the image, the word is knowledge and therefore you are looking at that flower with the word, the symbol, with knowledge and therefore you are not looking at the flower. Or, are you looking at it with a mind that is thinking about something else?

When you look at a flower without the word, without the image, and with a mind that is completely attentive, then what is the relationship between you and the flower? Have you ever done it? Have you ever looked at a flower without saying that is a rose? Have you ever looked at a flower completely, with total attention in which there is no word, no symbol, no naming of the flower and, therefore, complete attention? Till you do that, you have no relationship with the flower. To have any relationship with another or with the rock or with the leaf, one has to watch and to observe with complete attention. Then your relationship to that which you see is entirely different. Then there is no observer at all. There is only that. If you so observe, then there is no opinion, no judgement. It is what it is. Have you understood? Will you do it? Look at a flower that way. Do it, Sir, don't talk about it, but do it.

Student: If you have lots of time, how would you spend it, Sir?

Krishnamurti: I would do what I am doing. You see, if you love what you are doing, then you have all the leisure that you need in your life. Do you understand what I have said? You asked me what I would do if I had leisure. I said, I would do what I am doing; which is to go around different parts of the world, to talk, to see people and so on. I do it because I love to do it; not because I talk to a great many people and feel that I am very important. When you feel very important, you do not love what you are doing; you love yourself and not what you are doing. So, your concern should be not with what I am doing, but with what you are going to do. Right? I have told you what I am doing. Now you tell me what you will do, when you have plenty of leisure.

Student: I would get bored, sir.

Krishnamurti: You would get bored. Quite right. That is what most people are.

Student: How do I get rid of this boredom, sir?

Krishnamurti: Wait, listen. Most people are bored. Why? You asked how to get rid of boredom. Now find out. When you are by yourself for half an hour, you are bored. So you pick up a book, chatter, look at a magazine, go to a cinema, talk, do something. You occupy your mind with something. This is an escape from yourself. You have asked a question. Now, pay attention to what is being said. You get bored because you find yourself with yourself; and you have never found yourself with yourself. Therefore, you get bored. You say: Is that all I am? I am so small, I am so worried; I want to escape from all that. What you are is very boring, so you run away. But if you say, I am not going to be bored; I am going to find out why I am like this; I want to see what I am like actually then it is like looking at yourself in a mirror. There, you see very clearly what you are, what your face looks like. Then you say that you do not like your face; that you must be beautiful, you must look like a cinema actress. But if you were to look at yourself and say, "Yes, that is what I am; my nose is not very straight, my eyes are rather small, my hair is straight." You accept it. When you see what you are, there is no boredom. Boredom comes in only when you reject what you see and want to be something else. In the same way, when you can look at yourself inside and see exactly what you are, the seeing of it is not boring. It is extraordinarily interesting, because the more you see of it, the more there is to see. You can go deeper and deeper and wider and there is no end to it. In that, there is no boredom. If you can do that, then what you do is what you love to do, and when you love to do a thing, time does not exist. When you love to plant trees, you water them, look after them, protect them; when you know what you really love to do, you will see the days are too short. So you have to find out for yourself from now on, what you love to do; what you really want to do, not just be concerned with a career.

Student: How do you find out what you love to do, sir?

Krishnamurti: How do you find out what you love to do? You have to understand that it may be different from what you want to do. You may want to become a lawyer, because your father is a lawyer or because you see that by becoming a lawyer you can earn more money. Then you do not love what you do because you have a motive for doing something which will give you profit, which will make you famous. But if you love something, there is no motive. You do not use what you are doing for your own self-importance.

To find out what you love to do is one of the most difficult things. That is part of education. To find that out, you have to go into yourself very very deeply. It is not very easy. You may say: "I want to be a lawyer" and you struggle to be a lawyer, and then suddenly you find you do not want to be a lawyer. You would like to paint. But it is too late. You are already married. You already have a wife and children. You cannot give up your career, your responsibilities. So you feel frustrated, unhappy. Or you may say, "I really would like to paint," and you devote all your life to it, and suddenly find you are not a good painter and that what you really want to do is to be a pilot.

Right education is not to help you to find careers; for god's sake, throw that out of the window. Education is not merely gathering information from a teacher or learning mathematics from a book or learning historical dates of kings and customs, but education is to help you to understand the problems as they arise, and that requires a good mind—a mind that reasons, a mind that is sharp, a mind that has no belief. For belief is not fact. A man who believes in god is as superstitious as a man who does not believe in god. To find out you have to reason and you cannot reason if you already have an opinion, if you are prejudiced, if your mind has already come to a conclusion. So you need a good mind, a sharp, clear, definite, precise, healthy mind—not a believing mind, not a mind that follows authority. Right education is to help you to find out for yourself what you really, with all your heart, love to do. It does not matter what it is, whether it is to cook or to be a gardener, but it is something in which you have put your mind, your heart. Then you are really efficient, without becoming brutal. And this school should be a place where you are helped to find out for yourself through discussion, through listening, through silence, to find out, right through your life, what you really love to do.

Student: Sir, how can we know ourselves?

Krishnamurti: That is a very good question. Listen to me carefully. How do you know what you are? You understand my question? You look into the mirror for the first time and after a few days or few weeks, you look again and say, "That is me again." Right? So, by looking at the mirror every day, you begin to know your own face, and you say: "That is me." Now can you in the same way know what you are by watching yourself? Can you watch your gestures, the way you walk, the way you talk, the way you behave, whether you are hard, cruel, rough, patient? Then you begin to know yourself. You know yourself by watching yourself in the mirror of what you are doing, what you are thinking, what you are feeling. That is the mirror—the feeling, the doing, the thinking. And in that mirror you begin to watch yourself. The mirror says, this is the fact; but you do not like the fact. So, you want to alter it. You start distorting it. You do not see it as it is.

Now, as I said the other day, you learn when there is attention and silence. Learning is when you have silence and give complete attention. In that state, you begin to learn. Now, sit very quietly; not because I am asking you to sit quietly, but because that is the way to learn. Sit very quietly and be still not only physically, not only in your body, but also in your mind. Be very still and then in that stillness, attend. Attend to the sounds outside this building, the cock crowing, the birds, somebody coughing, somebody leaving; listen first to the things outside you, then listen to what is going on in your mind. And you will then see, if you listen very very attentively, in that silence, that the outside sound and the inside sound are the same.

9 / On Behaviour

One of the most difficult things in life is to find a way of behaviour that is not dictated by circumstances. Circumstances and people dictate, or force you to behave in a certain way. The way you conduct yourself, the way you eat, the way you talk, your moral, your ethical behaviour depend on where you find yourself and so your behaviour is constantly varying, constantly changing. This is so when you speak to your father, your mother or to your servant—your voice, your words, are quite different. The ways of behaviour are controlled by environmental influences, and by analysing behaviour you can almost predict what people will do or will not do.

Now can one ask oneself if one can behave the same inwardly, whatever the circumstances? Can one's behaviour spring from within and not depend on what people think of you or how they look at you? But that is difficult because one does not know what one is within. Within, a constant change is going on also. You are not what you were yesterday. Now can one find for oneself a way of behaviour which is not dictated by others or by society or by circumstances or by religious sanctions, a way of behaviour that does not depend on environment? I think one can find that out, if one knows what love is.

Do you know what love is? Do you know what it is to love people? To look after a tree, to brush a dog, comb it, feed it, means that you care for the tree, you feel great affection for the dog. I do not know whether you have noticed a tree in a street for which nobody cares; occasionally people look at it and pass it by. That tree is entirely different from a tree that is cared for in a garden, a tree you sit under, look at, on which you see the leaves, climb the branches. Such a tree grows with strength. When you look after a tree, when you give it water, manure; when you trim it, prune it, care for it, it has a different feeling altogether from the tree that grows by the roadside.

The feeling of care is the beginning of affection. You know, the more you look after things, the more sensitive you become. So there has to be affection, a sense of tenderness, kindliness, generosity. If there is such affection, then behaviour is dictated by that affection and is not dependent on environment, circumstance, or people. And to find that affection is one of the most difficult things—to be really affectionate whether people are kind to you or not kind to you, whether they talk to you roughly, or whether they are irritated with you. I think children have it. You all have it when you are young. You feel very friendly with one another, with people.

You love to pat a dog. You look occasionally at things and you also smile easily. But as you grow older, all this disappears. And so to have affection right through life is one of the most difficult things and without it life becomes very empty. You may have children, you may have a nice house, a car and all the rest of it, but without affection life is like a flower that has no scent. And it is part of education, is it not, to come to this affection, from which there is great joy, from which alone love can come?

With most of us love is possessiveness. Where there is jealousy, envy, it breeds cruelty, it breeds hatred. Love can only exist and flower when there is no hate, no envy, no ambition. Without love, life is like the barren earth, arid, hard, brutal. But the moment there is affection it is like the earth which blossoms with water, with rain, with beauty. One has to learn all this when one is very young, not when one is old for then it is too late. Then you become prisoners of society, of environment, of husband, wife, office. Find out for yourself if you can behave with affection. Can you go to your class punctually because you feel you do not want to keep people waiting? Can you stop shouting while you are together because there are other people watching you, being with you?

When behaviour, politeness, consideration are superficial and without affection they have no meaning. But if there is affection, kindliness, consideration, then, out of that, comes politeness, good manners, consideration for others, which means really that one is thinking less and less about oneself, and that is one of the most difficult things in life. When one is not concerned with oneself, then one is really a free human being. Then one can look at the skies, the mountains, the hills, the waters, the birds, the flowers, with a fresh mind, with a great sense of affection. Right? Now, ask questions.

Student: If there is jealousy in love, is there not also sacrifice in love?

Krishnamurti: Is there not also sacrifice in love? Love can never sacrifice. What do you mean by using that word "sacrifice?" Giving up? Doing things you do not want to do? Is that what you mean? I sacrifice myself for my country, because I love my country. I sacrifice myself because I love my parents. Is that what you mean? Now, is that love? Can love exist when you have to force yourself to do something for others? I wonder if you understand the word "sacrifice." Why do you use that word? You know, the words, "responsibility," "duty," "sacrifice," are dreadful words. When you love somebody there is no responsibility, there is no duty, there is no sacrifice. You do things because you love. And you cannot love if you are thinking about yourself. When you are thinking about yourself, then you come first and the other is second; then, to love him, you sacrifice yourself. Then it is not love. It is a bargain. Do you understand?

Student: To learn and to love; are they separate or are they connected, sir?

Krishnamurti: Do you know what it means to love and do you know what it means to learn?

Student: I know what it is to learn.

Krishnamurti: I wonder. I do not say you do not know. I am just asking you. Do you know what it means to learn? You know what it means to acquire knowledge. You hear the teacher tell you certain facts and you store what you hear in your mind, in your brain. This storing up process is what we call learning. Is that not so?

Student: In a way.

Krishnamurti: In a way. But what is the other way? You have an experience, you walk up the hills and slip and hurt yourself and you have learnt something from that. You meet a friend and he hurts you and you have learnt from that. You read a newspaper and you have learnt from that. So, your learning generally consists of adding more and more information. Now is that learning? There is another form of learning—that is, learning as you go along, never accumulating. And then from that to act, to think. Do you understand what it is to learn in doing? This does not mean having learnt and then doing. They are two different states, are they not? There is a state where I have learnt and from that knowledge I act, and there is learning as I am doing. The two are completely different. When I have learnt and then do, it is mechanical, whereas learning from doing is non-mechanical. It is always fresh. Therefore, learning as I am doing is never boring; it is never tiring, whereas to do, having learnt, becomes mechanical. That is why you all get bored with your learning. Do you understand? So now you know what learning means. Learning is doing, so that in the very act of doing you are learning. Now, what is love?

Love is a feeling in which there is gentleness, quietness, tenderness, consideration, in which there is beauty. In love there is no ambition, there is no jealousy. Now you had asked whether learning and love are not similar. You had asked that question, had you not?

Student: Are they connected?

Krishnamurti: What do you say? You have understood what we mean by love, what we mean by learning. Are they connected?

Student: In a way.

Krishnamurti: Tell me in which way. May I help you? They are connected because both require an activity which is non-mechanical. Do you understand? Learning as I am doing is non-mechanical. But in love which becomes mechanical there is no learning. Love in which there is ambition, conflict, greed, envy, jealousy, anger, ambition, is not love. When there is no ambition, no jealousy, then there is a very active principle. It is renewing itself all the time, it is fresh. There is, in both learning and love, a movement of freshness, a movement which is spontaneous, which is not held by circumstances. It is a free movement. So there is a tenuous, delicate connection between the two. But to learn and to love there must be a great deal of affection. There is a great similarity in both when there is attention, which is not merely a conclusion. So if you are attending, attending to what you are thinking, out of that, there is affection, out of that there is learning.

Student: How can we live our life, sir?

Krishnamurti: First of all, do you know what your life is, to live it? I am not being funny. I am just asking. To live your life, you must know what your life is and to find out what your life is, you have to again examine. Your life is not what your father or mother, your society, your teacher, your neighbour, your religion, your politician tell you it is. Do not say: "No". It is so. Your life is made up of influences—political, religious, social, economic, climatic—all these influences converge in

you and you say: "That is life. I must live it." You can only
live your life when you understand all these influences, and
through understanding them begin to discover your own way
of thinking and living. Then you do not have to ask: "How
can I live my life?" Then you live it. But, first, you must
understand all the influences. The influence of society, the
political speeches, the politicians, the climate, the food, the
books you read are influencing you all the time. You have to
ask whether it is at all possible to be free of these influences.
And that is one of the most demanding enquiries. And after
enquiring, examining, you have to understand, to find a way
of life that is neither yours nor anybody's. It is then life. Then
you are living.

Now, in all this, what is important? The first thing is not
to lead a mechanical life. You understand what I mean by a
mechanical life? It is doing something because somebody tells
you to do it, or because you feel that it is the right thing to
do, so you repeat, repeat, and gradually, your brain, your
mind, your body becomes dull, heavy, stupid. So, do not lead
a life of routine. You may have to go to the office. You may
have to pass an examination, to study. But do it all with a
freshness, with eagerness; and you can only do it with freshness and with vigour, when you are learning. And you cannot
learn if you are not attentive.

The second thing is, to be very gentle, to be very kind, not
to hurt people. You have to look at people, help people, be
generous, be considerate.

There must be love, otherwise, your life is empty. You
understand? You may have everything you want: husband,

cars, children, wife; but life will be like an empty desert. You may be very clever, you might have a very good position, be a good lawyer, a good engineer, a marvelous administrator, but, without love, you are a dead human being. So do not do anything mechanical. Find out what it is to love people, to love dogs, the sky, the blue hills and the river. Love and feel.

Then you must also know what meditation is, what it is to have a very still, a very quiet mind, not a chattering mind. And it is only such a mind that can know the real religious mind. And without the religious mind, without that feeling, life is like a flower that has no fragrance, a river bed that has never known the rippling waters over it, it is like the earth that has never grown a tree, a bush, a flower.

TALKS TO
TEACHERS

1 / On Right Education

Krishnamurti: It is our intention in places like Rishi Valley in the South and Rajghat in the North to create an environment, a climate, where one can bring about, if it is at all possible, a new human being. Do you know the history of these two schools? They have been running for thirty years or more. The purpose, the aim and drive of these schools is to equip the child with the most excellent technological proficiency so that he may function with clarity and efficiency in the modern world, and far more important to create the right climate so that the child may develop fully as a complete human being. This means giving him the opportunity to flower in goodness so that he is rightly related to people, things and ideas, to the whole of life. To live is to be related. There is no right relationship to anything if there is not the right feeling for beauty, a response to nature, to music and art, a highly developed aesthetic sense.

I think it is fairly clear that competitive education and the development of the student in that process is very destructive. I do not know how deeply one has grasped the significance of this. If one has, then what is right education? I think it is clear that the pattern which we now cultivate and call education, which is conformity to society, is very, very destructive. In its ambitious activities, it is frustrating in the extreme. And what we have so far considered, both in the West and East, as a development within this process, is culture. It is the inevitable invitation to sorrow. The perception of the truth of that is essential. If it is very clear, and if one has abandoned that voluntarily, not as a reaction, but just as a leaf falls away from the tree, a dropping away, then what is flowering, what is right education? Do you educate the student to conform, to adjust, to fit into the system or do you educate him to comprehend, to see very clearly the whole significance of all that and, at the same time, help him to read and write? If you teach him to read and write within the present system of frustration, then the flowering of the mind is impeded. The question then is, if one drops this competitive education, can the mind be educated at all in the ordinary accepted sense of the word? Or does education consist really in taking ourselves and the student away from the social structure of frustration and desire and, at the same time giving him information about mathematics, physics, and so on? After all, if the teacher and the student are stripped of all this monstrous confusion, what is there to be educated about? All that you can teach the student is how to read and write, how to calculate, design, remember and communicate facts and opinions about facts.

So, what is the function of education and is there a particular method of education? Do you teach the student a technique so that he becomes proficient and in that very proficiency develops a sense of ambition? By teaching him a technique in order to find a job, you also burden him with its implications of success and frustration. He wants to be successful in life and he also wants to be a peaceful man. His whole life is a contradiction. The greater the contradiction, the greater the tension. This is a fact. When there is suppression in contradiction, there is greater outward activity. You give the student a technique and at the same time develop in him this extraordinary imbalance, this extreme contradiction which leads to frustration and despair. The more he develops his capacity in technique, the greater his ambition and the greater the frustration. You are educating him to have a technique which is going to lead to his despair. So the question is, can you help him not to drift into contradiction? He will drift into it if you do not help him to love the thing which he is doing.

You see, if the student loves geometry, loves it as an end in itself, he is so completely absorbed in it that he has no ambition. He really loves geometry and that is an enormous delight. Therefore he flowers in it. How will you help the student to love, in this way, a thing which the student has not yet discovered for himself?

If you are asked, as a teacher, what the intention of this school is would you be able to reply? I want to know what you are all trying to do, what you intend the student to be? Are you trying to shape him, condition him, force him in certain directions? Are you trying to teach the student mathematics, physics, giving him some information so that he is proficient technologically and can do well in a future career? Thousands of schools are doing this, all over the world—trying to make the student excellent technologically so that he becomes a good scientist, engineer, physicist and so on. Or are you trying to do something much more here? If it is much more, what is it?

We must be very clear in ourselves what we want, clear what a human being must be—the total human being, not just the technological human being. If we concentrate very much on examinations, on technological information, on making the child clever, proficient in acquiring knowledge, while we neglect the other side, then the child will grow up into a one-sided human being. When we talk about a total human being, we mean not only a human being with inward understanding, with a capacity to explore, to examine his inward being, his inward state and the capacity of going beyond it, but also someone who is good in what he does outwardly. The two must go together. That is the real issue in education—to see that when the child leaves the school, he is well established in goodness, both outwardly and inwardly.

There must be a starting point from which we function so that we will cultivate not only the technological side but also uncover the deeper layers, the deeper fields of the human mind. I will put it another way. If you concentrate on making the student excellent in technology and neglect the other side, as we generally do, what happens to such a human being? If you concentrate on making the student a perfect dancer or a perfect mathematician, what happens? He is not just that, he is something more. He is jealous, angry, frustrated, in despair, ambitious. So you will create a society in which there is always disorder, because you are emphasizing technology and proficiency in one field and neglecting the other field. However perfect a man may be technologically, he is always in contradiction in his social relationships. He is always in battle with his neighbour.

So technology cannot produce a perfect or a good society. It may produce a great society, where there is no poverty, where there is material equality and so on. A great society is not necessarily a good society. A good society implies order. Order does not mean trains running on time, mail delivered regularly.It means something else. For a human being, order means order within himself. And such order will inevitably bring about a good society. Now from which centre are we to start?

Do you understand my question? If I neglect the inner and accentuate technology, whatever I do will be one-sided. So I must find a way, I must bring about a movement which will cover both. So far, we have separated the two and having separated them, we have emphasized the one and neglected the other. What we are now trying to do is to join both of them together. If there is proper education, the student will not treat them as two separate fields. He will be able to move in both as one movement. Right? In making himself technologically perfect, he will also make himself a worthwhile human being. Does this convey something or not?

A river is not always the same, the banks vary, and the water can be used industrially or for various other purposes, but it is still water. Why have we separated the technological world and the other world? We have said: "If we could make the technological world perfect, we would have food, clothes, shelter for everybody, so let us concern ourselves with the technological." And there are also those who are concerned only with the inner world. They emphasize the so-called inner world, and become more and more isolated, more and more self-centered, more and more vague, pursuing their own beliefs, dogmas and visions. There is this tremendous division and we say we must somehow bring these two together. So having divided life into the outer and inner, we now try to integrate them. I think that way also leads to more conflict. Whereas if we could find a centre, a movement, an approach which does not divide, we would function in both equally.

What is the movement that is supremely intelligent? I am using the word "intelligent," not clever, not intuitive, not derived from knowledge, information, experience. What is the movement that understands all these divisions, all these conflicts; and that very understanding creates the movement of intelligence?

We see in the world two movements going on, the deep religious movement which man has always sought and which has become Catholicism, Protestantism, Hinduism, and this wordly movement of technology, a world of computers and automation that give man more leisure. The religious movement is very feeble and very few are pursuing it. The technological has become stronger and stronger and man is getting lost in it, becoming more mechanical and therefore man tries to escape from this mechanism, tries to discover something new—in painting, in music, in art, in the theatre. And the religious, if there are any, say "That is the wrong way" and move away to a world of their own. They do not see the insufficiency, the immaturity, the mechanical way of both. Now, can we see that both of these are insufficient? If we can see that, then we are beginning to perceive a non-mechanistic movement which will cover both.

If I had a child to be educated I would help him to see the mechanical and the insufficient processes of both ways and in the very examination of the insufficiency of both as they operate in him, there would be born the intelligence which has come into being through examination.

Sirs, look at those flowers, the brilliancy, the beauty of them. Now, how am I, as a teacher, to help the student to see the flowers and also be very good at mathematics? If I am only concerned with the flowers and I am not good at mathematics, something is wrong with me. If I am only concerned with mathematics, then also something is wrong with me.

You cannot cultivate technological information, become perfect in it first and then say you must also study the other. By giving your heart to years of acquiring knowledge you have already destroyed something in you—the feeling and the capacity to look. By emphasizing one or the other you become insensitive and the essence of intelligence is sensitivity.

So, the quality which we want the child to have is the highest form of sensitivity. Sensitivity is intelligence; it does not come from books. If you spend forty years in learning mathematics but cannot look at those flowers and also study mathematics. If there is a movement of that intelligence it will cover both fields. Now how are you and I, as a community of teachers, going to create that movement of sensitivity in the child?

The student must be free. Otherwise he cannot be sensitive. If he is not free in the study of mathematics, enjoying mathematics, giving his heart to it, which is freedom, he cannot study it adequately. And to look at those flowers, to look at that beauty, he must also be free. So there must be freedom first. That means I must help that boy to be free. Freedom implies order, freedom does not mean allowing the boy to do what he likes, to come to lunch and to class when he likes.

In examining, working, in learning, one understands that the highest form of sensitivity is intelligence. That sensitivity, that intelligence can come about only in freedom, but to convey that to a child requires a great deal of intelligence on our part. I would like to help him to be free and yet at the same time have order and discipline, without conformity. To examine anything one must have not only freedom but discipline. This discipline is not something from outside which has been imposed upon the child and according to which he tries to conform. In the very examination of these two processes—the technological and the religious, there is attention and therefore discipline. Therefore one asks, "How can we help that boy or girl to be free completely and yet highly disciplined, not through fear, not through conformity, not partially free but completely free and yet highly disciplined at the same time?" Not one first and then the other. They both go together.

Now, how are we to do this? Do we clearly see that freedom is absolutely essential, and that freedom does not mean doing what one likes? You cannot do what you like, because you are always in relationship in life with others. See the necessity and importance of being completely free and yet highly disciplined without conformity. See that your beliefs, your ideas, your ideologies are secondhand. You have to see all that and see that you must be absolutely free. Otherwise you cannot function as a human being.

Now I wonder if you see this as an idea or as a fact, as factual as this inkpot. How will you, as a community of teachers, when you see the importance of the child being completely free and also realise that there must be discipline and order—how will you help him so that he flowers in freedom and order? Your shouting at the child is not going to do it; your beating the child is not going to do it, your comparing him to another is not going to do it. Any form of compulsion, bullying, or system of giving him marks or no marks is not going to do it.

If you see the importance of the boy being free and at the same time highly orderly, and if you see that punishment or cajoling him is not going to produce anything, will you completely drop all that in yourself?

The old method has not produced freedom. It has made man comply and adjust, but if you see that freedom is absolutely necessary and therefore order is essential, these methods which we have used for centuries must drop away.

The difficulty is that you are used to old methods and suddenly you are deprived of them. So you are confronted with a problem about which you have to think in a totally different way. It is your problem. It is your responsibility. You are confronted with this issue. You cannot possibly employ the old methods, because you have seen that the boy must be totally free and yet there must be order. So what has happened to you who have, so far, accepted and functioned with an old formula? You have thrown out the formula and are looking at the problem anew, are you not? You are looking at the problem with a fresh mind which is free.

Teacher: To see, does one always have to be in that state?

Krishnamurti: If you do not see it now but demand to see it always, that is nonsense. The seeing once is the seed put in the earth, that will flower. But if you say that you must see it always, then you are back to the old formula.

Look what has happened: the old patterns of thinking with regard to teaching and freedom and order have been taken away from you. Therefore you are looking at problems differently. The difference is that your mind is now free to look, free to examine the issue of freedom and order. Now how will you convey to the child that you are not going to punish him, not going to reward him and yet he must be totally free and orderly?

Teacher: I think the teacher has the same problem as the child. He needs to operate from a field where he feels freedom and discipline go together. In his present thinking, he separates order and freedom. He says freedom is against order and order is against freedom.

Krishnamurti: I think we are missing something. When you see that the old methods of punishment and reward are dead, your mind becomes much more active. Because you have to solve this problem, your mind is alive. If it is alive, it will be in contact with the issue.

Because you are free and understand freedom, you will be punctual in your class and from freedom you will talk to the student and not from an idea. To talk from an idea, a formula, a concept is one thing, but to talk from an actual fact which you have seen—that the student must be free and therefore orderly—is totally different. When you as a teacher are free and orderly you are already communicating it, not only verbally but non-verbally and the student knows it immediately.

Once you see the fact that punishment and reward in any form are destructive, you never go back to them. By throwing them out, you yourself are disciplined and that discipline has come out of the freedom of examination. You communicate to the child the fact of that and not any idea. Then you have communicated to him not only verbally, but at a totally different level.

2 / On the Long Vision

I think most of us know what is happening in the world—
the threat of war, the nuclear bomb, the many tensions and
conflicts that have brought about new crises. It seems to me
that a totally different kind of mind is necessary to meet these
challenges. A mind that is not specialised, not trained only in
technology, that is not merely seeking prosperity, but that can
meet challenges adequately, completely. And it seems to me
that that is the function of education, that is the function of a
school.

Everywhere—in Europe, Russia, America, Japan and here
—they are turning out technicians, scientists, educators. These
specialists are incapable of meeting the enormously complex
challenge of life. They are utterly incapable and yet they are
the people who rule the world as the politician, as the scientist.
They are specialists in their fields and their guidance, their

leadership has obviously failed and is failing. They are merely responding to the immediate. You see, we are thinking in terms of the immediate, the immediacy of events. We are concerned with the immediate responses of a country that is very poor, like India, or the immediate responses of the enormous prosperity of the West. Everyone is thinking in terms of doing something immediately. I think one has to take a long view of the whole problem and I do not think a specialist can do this because specialists always think in terms of action which is immediate. Though immediate action is necessary, I think the function of education is to bring about a mind that will not only act in the immediate but go beyond.

Throughout the world the authoritarian governments, the priests, the professors, the analysts, the psychologists, everybody is concerned with controlling or shaping or directing the mind and, therefore, there is very little freedom. The real issue is to find out how to live in a world that is so compulsively authoritarian, so brutal and tyrannical, not only in the immediate relationships but in social relationships, how to live in such a world with the extraordinary capacity to meet its demands and also to be free. I feel education of the right kind should cultivate the mind not to fall into grooves of habit, however worthy or noble, however technologically necessary, but to have a mind that is extraordinarily alive, not with knowledge, not with experience, but alive. Because often the more knowledge one has, the less alert the brain is.

I am not against knowledge. There is a difference between learning and acquiring knowledge. Learning ceases when there is only accumulation of knowledge. There is learning only when there is no acquisition at all. When knowledge becomes all important learning ceases. The more I add to knowledge the more secure, the more assured the mind becomes, and, therefore it ceases to learn. Learning is never an additive process. When one is learning, it is an active process. Whereas acquiring knowledge is merely gathering information and storing it up. So I think there is a difference between acquiring knowledge and learning. Education throughout the world is merely the acquisition of knowledge and therefore the mind becomes dull and ceases to learn. The mind is merely acquiring. The acquisition dictates the conduct of life and, therefore, limits experience. Whereas learning is limitless.

Can one, in a school, not only acquire knowledge, which is necessary for living in this world, but also have a mind that is constantly learning? The two are not in contradiction. In a school, when knowledge becomes all important, learning becomes a contradiction. Education should be concerned with the totality of life and not with the immediate responses to the immediate challenges.

Let us see what is involved in the two. If one is living in terms of the immediate, responding to the immediate challenge, the immediate is constantly repeated in different ways. In one year it will be war, the next year it may be revolution, in the third year industrial unrest; if one is living in terms of the immediate, life becomes very superficial. But you may say that that is enough because that is all we need to care about. That is one way of taking life. If you live that way it is an empty life. You can fill it with cars, books, sex, drink, more clothes, but it is shallow and empty. A man living an empty life, a shallow life, is always trying to escape; and escape means delusion, more gods, more beliefs, more dogmas, more authoritarian attitudes, or more football, more sex, more television. The immediate responses of those who live in the immediate are extraordinarily empty, futile, miserable. This is not my feeling or prejudice; you can watch it. You may say that is enough, or you may say that that is not good enough. So there must be the long vision, though I must of course act in the immediate, do something about it when the house is burning, but that is not the end of action. There must be something else, and how can one pursue that something else without bringing in authority, books, priests? Can one wipe them all out and pursue the other? If one pursues the other, this immediacy will be answered in a greater and more vital way. So, what do you, as a human being and also as an educator, a teacher, what do you feel about it?

I do not want you to agree with me. But if you have exercised your brain, if you have observed world events, if you have watched your own inclinations, your own demands, persuasions, if you have seen the whole state of man and his quivering despair, how do you respond? What is your action, your way of looking at it all? Forget that you are in a school. We are talking as human beings.

Teacher: In meeting an immediate challenge, especially as one grows older, one seems to bring in a sense of anxiety. Is there, as one grows older, another approach?

Krishnamurti: What do you mean by "getting older?" Older in terms of doing a job? Older in terms of routine, boredom?

What do you mean by age? What makes you old? The organism wears out—why? Is it due to disease, or is it because there is repetition like a machine going on over and over again? The psyche is never alive; it is merely functioning in habit. So it reduces the body quickly to old age. Why does the psyche become old, or need it ever get old? I do not think it need ever get old. And is old age only a habit? Have you noticed old people, how they eat, how they talk? And is it possible to keep the psyche extraordinarily young, alive, innocent? Is it possible for the psyche to be alive and never for a second lose its vitality through habit, through security, through family, through responsibility? Of course it is possible, which means that you must destroy everything you build. That is what I mean by the long vision. You have an experience, pleasant or unpleasant, that leaves a mark, and the mind lives in that: "I have had such a marvellous experience" or "I have had such a sad life," and there is a decaying in itself. So, experience, and the living in experience, is decay.

Let us come back to my question. As a human being, living in this society, in a world which is demanding immediate action, what is your response to the immediate challenge? The immediate challenge is always asking you to respond immediately, and you are caught in that. How do you, as a parent, as a teacher, as a citizen, respond to it? For, according to your response, you are caught in it. Whether you respond consciously or unconsciously, the effect of that will be on the psyche.

Teacher: Is there a way by which this long vision becomes an actuality, as actual as the immediate?

Krishnamurti: Of course. Because the immediate is the actual. There is the nuclear bomb—the Russian, the American, the French scientists are inventing ways of producing cheap atom bombs—they may blow themselves to bits. Why should you respond to it? The nuclear bomb is the result of a long series of events—nationalism, industrialism, class differences, greed, envy, hate, ambition—all these have produced the nuclear bomb. You reply without understanding it—that America or Russia should be stopped from producing nuclear bombs, and you call that an actual response. Without answering the total, what is the good of replying to the fragments of the problem? So, if this is the actual and you see that the actual produces such immature responses, then you must pursue the other. Knowing that you must respond to the immediate and also that you must have long vision, how do you bring this about as an educator? Nobody is concerned with the other; no educator is concerned with the long vision, the long view. Education today is concerned only with the immediate. But if you are dissatisfied with the immediate, then how would you pursue that and not neglect this? Do you see the urgency of it?

Shall I put the problem differently? How can one keep the mind young, never let it grow old and never say, "I have had enough," and seek a corner to stay in and stagnate? That is the tendency and that is the actual fact. To get a position is difficult, but once you have got it, you stagnate. Everything about the world is destroying the long vision. Books, newspapers, politicians, priests, everything influences you, and how does one walk out of it all? You are being contaminated and yet you have to function and you cannot walk out of it.

Life is destruction, life is love, life is creation. We know none of it. It is a tremendous thing. Now how would you translate all this into education?

Teacher: Is it possible to pursue one vision at the cost of another? Is it possible to do away with the short vision?

Krishnamurti: The problem is not to run away from all this misery or to see how to combine the two. You cannot combine the little with the big; the big has to take in the little.

Teacher: But is it not better to follow the little in the beginning and come to the big later?

Krishnamurti: Never. If you say the little is the first step, then you are lost, you are caught in the little. Think it out for yourself. If you accept the little, then where are you? You will be caught, won't you—little family, little house, little husband, little money, little clothes? You have made the little important, the little first and so you have little responsibility in society. You are all so terribly respectable. Why do you put the little first? Because that is the easiest way.

Teacher: How does one grasp the little and understand it?

Krishnamurti: You can only grasp the big, the little is not at all important, but you have made it important.

It is a very delicate thing, a subtle thing, to have capacity and not to be a slave to it, to respond immediately to things you have to respond to, and to have this extraordinary depth and height and width.

Deny the little. Do you know what it is to deny? Deny not because you have got the long vision but because what is denied is false.

3 / On Action

Krishnamurti: Shall we consider the question of immediacy of action? Action is pressing on each one of us, and there must be the long vision which includes the immediacy; but the immediacy does not include the larger, the wider, the deeper. Most people throughout the world who are intellectual and learned seem to be caught in the immediate responses to immediate challenges. More scientists, more engineers, more technicians are needed and education is geared to produce them. The immediate demand is accepted and answered and so one loses, I think, a larger perspective and therefore one's mind and body and emotions become very shallow and empty. If one actually realises all this, not verbally, but with a direct perception, how is a teacher to educate a student to have not only technical knowledge, the know-how, but also a wider, deeper understanding of life?

How will you translate this into action in education? Is that not what you have come here to do? How do you set about it, if you have not already done it? I believe, here in Rishi Valley, the origin of the school was to bring about a different kind of education. It was not only to provide the child with knowledge but to make him understand that knowledge is not the end of life; that it is necessary to be sensitive to trees, to beauty, to know what it is to love, to be kind, to be generous. Now how would you set about it?

It seems at first absolutely necessary that there should be a few who have this feeling, and by their enthusiasm, understanding, capacity, not only to impart knowledge but also to see beyond the hills. If I were here and I felt this urgency that a student must academically be most proficient, and also that he must know how to dance, sing, look at the trees, see the mountains, know how to look at a woman without the usual sexual attitude and consider the extraordinary beauty of life, know sorrow and go beyond sorrow—if I were here, how would I set about it?

If I were here and my sole job was that, I would not leave any one of you alone. I would discuss with you the way you talk, dress, look, behave, eat; I would be at it all the time—and probably you would call me a tyrant and talk of democracy and freedom. I do not think it is a question of democracy, tyranny and freedom. You see, this brings up the question of authority. We have talked about it a great deal in this place, on and off, whenever I have come; but let us discuss authority again.

To me, authority is terrible, destructive. The quality of

authority is tyrannical—the authority of the priest, the police-man, the authority of law. Those are all outward authorities. There is also the inward authority of knowledge, of one's own dignity, of one's own experience which dictates certain atti-tudes to life. All this breeds authority and without exercising this authority, you have to look after the child, to see that he has good taste, that he puts on the right clothes, eats properly, has a certain dignity in speech, in the way he walks; you have also to teach him to play games, not competitively and ruth-lessly, but for the fun of it. To awaken in him all this without authority is extremely difficult and because of its difficulty, you resort to authority.

One must have discipline in the school. Now, can you bring about discipline without exercising authority? Children must come to meals regularly, not talk incessantly at meal time, everything must be in proportion, in freedom and affec-tion; and there must be a certain non-authoritarian awakening of self-respect.

To give knowledge which does not become an end in itself and to educate the mind to have a long vision, a wide compre-hension of life, is not possible if education is based on author-ity.

Teacher: It is extremely difficult to bring about an inner orderliness in the child without discipline, without restraint and authority. Adults are in a different position from children.

Krishnamurti: I wonder if that is so. We are conditioned and children are being conditioned. Can education bring about a revolutionary mind? The difficulty is that this has to begin at a very tender age, not when children are fourteen or older.

By then they are already formed and destroyed but if they came to you very young what would you do to encourage a feeling that there are other things than mere sex, money and position?

Besides giving the child information as knowledge, how would you show him that the world is not only the immediate but that there are other things far greater? First, you and I must feel this, not merely because I talk about it or you talk about it. I must be burning with it, and if I am burning with it, how do I communicate it without influencing the child? Because when I influence, I destroy the child; I make him conform to the image I have. So I must realise, though I feel very strongly about all this, that in my relationship with the student, however young, I must not encourage an imitative attitude and action. This is all extremely difficult. If I love somebody, I want him to be different, to do things differently, to look at life, to feel the beauty of the earth. Can I show him all this without influence, without breeding the imitative instinct?

Teacher: Before we come to help the child without influencing him, is there an approach which we can establish in ourselves, because in our lives there seem to be so many contradictions?

Krishnamurti: In order to establish it—one must change, remove the contradictions, wipe out destructive feelings. That may take many days or perhaps no time at all. We say that can be done through analysis, through awareness, through questioning, enquiring, probing. All that involves time. But time is a danger. Because the moment we look to time to change, it is really a continuation of what has been. If I have to enquire into my mind and be aware of my activities and my conditioning and my demands and each day probe, all that entails time. Time as a means to mutation is illusion. And when I introduce time into the problem of mutation, then mutation is postponed, because then time is merely a further continuation of my desire to go on as I am. Time is necessary to learn French. The time taken to learn French is not an illusion, but to bring about a psychological mutation, a psychical change in myself through time is an illusion, because it encourages laziness, postponement, a sense of achievement, vanity. All that is implied in the employment of time when I use time as a means to mutation. So, if I do not look to time at all for mutation, then what happens?

It is a marvellous thing. All religious people have seen time as a means of change and actually we find mutation can only be out of time, not through time.

Teacher: Does that not apply to all creative action?

Krishnamurti: Of course it does. So can my mind refuse to use time and deny time as a means to mutation? Do you see the beauty of it? Then what takes place?

The thing which I want changed has been put together through time, it is the result of time, and I deny time. Therefore I deny the whole thing and therefore mutation has taken place. I do not know if you see this. It is not a verbal trick.

Have you understood it? If I deny my conditioning as a Hindu, which is the result of time, and I deny time, I deny the whole thing. I am out of it. If I deny ritual—the Christian, Hindu or Buddhist—deny it because it is the product of time,

I am out. I do not have to ask how to bring about mutation. The thing itself is the result of time and I deny time—it is finished.

So the mind in which mutation has taken place, that mind can then instruct, can look, can bring about a definite series of environmental actions. One cannot deny the use of time for acquiring knowledge but does time exist anywhere else?

Teacher: Even in activities we need time, we seem to do things in a sloppy way and therefore time hangs heavily. If the understanding of time in all these things is as simple as this, why are we not able to get out of it?

Krishnamurti: But if you give your whole attention, not to mutation through time but to denying time, you would then be in a position to teach in a totally different way. The boys and girls are here to acquire knowledge and if you can impart this knowledge with attention which is not using time to convey information, then you are quickening their minds.

That is what I am interested in, which is, to awaken the mind, to keep the mind tremendously alive. We say the mind can be kept alive through knowledge and therefore we pour in knowledge which only dulls the mind. A mind that functions in time is still a limited mind. But a mind which does not function in time is extraordinarily alert, is tremendously alive and can impart its aliveness to a mind which is still seeking, enquiring, innocent. So we have discovered something new. You and I have discovered something. I have imparted something to you. Together we have found that the mind functions in time and the mind is the result of time. In that state, the mind can only give information. Such a mind is limited. But a mind that is not functioning, thinking in terms of time, though it uses time, will quicken the mind of another and therefore knowledge will not destroy. You see, such a mind is in a state of learning, not acquiring. Therefore it is everlastingly alive; such a mind is young.

Some of the boys in this school are already old, because they are merely concerned with acquiring knowledge, not with learning. And learning is out of time. Now, how will you set about quickening the mind, keeping it astonishingly alive all the time?

You have to understand the quality of a mind in which mutation has taken place. It has taken place the moment you deny time. You have thrown the whole past out. You are no longer a Hindu, a Christian. Now how will such a mind in which mutation has taken place instruct, translate its action? How will it act in giving knowledge which involves time, and yet keep the mind of the child in a state of intense aliveness? Find out.

4 / On the True Denial

Teacher: In one of your talks to the children you said that when a problem arises one should solve it immediately. How is one to do this?

Krishnamurti: To solve a problem immediately, you have to understand the problem. Is the understanding of a problem a matter of time or is it a matter of intensity of perception, an intensity of seeing? Let us say that I have a problem: I am vain. It is a problem with me in the sense that it creates a conflict, a contradiction within me. It is a fact that I am vain and there is also another fact that I do not want to be vain. Firstly, I have to understand the fact that I am vain. I have to live with that fact. I must not only be intensely aware of the fact but comprehend it fully. Now, is comprehension a matter of time? I can see the fact immediately, can't I? And the immediacy of perception, of seeing, dissolves the fact. When I see a cobra there is immediate action. But I do not see vanity in the same way —when I see vanity either I like it and therefore I continue with it, or I do not want it because it creates conflict. If it does not create conflict there is no problem.

Perception and understanding are not of time. Perception is a matter of intensity of seeing, a seeing that is total. What is the nature of seeing something totally? What gives one the capacity, the energy, the vitality, the drive, to deal with something immediately, with all one's undivided energy? The moment you have divided energy you have conflict and therefore there is no seeing, there is no perception of something total. Now, what gives you the energy to make you jump when you see a cobra? What are the processes that make the organic as well as the psychological, the whole being, jump, so that there is no hesitation, so that the reaction is immediate? What has gone into that immediacy? Several things have gone into that action which is immediate: fear, natural protection, which must be there, the knowledge that the cobra is a deadly thing.

Now, why have we not the same energetic action with regard to the dissolution of vanity? I am taking vanity as an example. There are several reasons that have gone into my lack of energy. I like vanity; the world is based on it; it is the basis of the social pattern; it gives me a certain sense of vitality, a certain quality of dignity and aloofness, a sense that I am a little better than another. All this prevents that energy which is necessary to dissolve vanity. Now, either I analyse all the reasons which have prevented my action, prevented my having energy to deal with vanity, or I see immediately. Analysis is a process of time and a process of postponement. While I am analysing, vanity continues and time is not going to end it. So I have to see vanity totally and I lack the energy to see. Now, to gather the dissipated energy requires a gathering not only when I am confronted with a problem such as vanity, but a gathering all the time, even when there is no problem. We do not have problems all the time. There are moments when we have no problems. If at those moments we are gathering energy, gathering in the sense of being aware, then, when the problem arises, we can meet it and not go through the process of analysis.

Teacher: There is another difficulty: when there is no problem, and no gathering of this energy, some form of mentation is going on.

Krishnamurti: There is a waste of energy in mere repetition, reaction to memory, reaction to experience. If you observe your own mind you will see that a pleasurable incident keeps on repeating itself. You want to go back to it, you want to think about it, so it gathers momentum. When the mind is aware there is no wastage, is it possible to let that momentum, to let that thought flower? Which means never to say, "This is right or wrong", but to live the thought over, to have a feeling in which the thought can flourish so that by itself it will come to an end.

Should we approach the problem differently? We have been talking about creating a generation with a new quality of mind. How do we do this? If I were a teacher here, it would be my concern—and a good educator obviously has this concern at heart—to bring about a new mind, a new sensitivity, a new feeling for the trees, the skies, the heavens, the streams, to bring into being a new consciousness, not the old consciousness remoulded into a new shape. I mean a totally new mind, uncontaminated by the past. If that is my concern, how do I set about it?

First of all, is it possible to bring about such a new mind? Not a mind which is a continuity of the past in a new mould but a mind that is uncontaminated. Is it feasible, or must the past continue through the present to be modified and be put into a new mould? In which case there is no new generation, it is the older generation repeated in a new form.

I think it is possible to create a new generation. And I ask: How am I, not only to experience this within myself, but to express it to the student?

If I see something experimentally in myself I cannot miss expressing it to the student. Surely it is not a question of I and the other, but a mutual thing, isn't it?

Now how do I bring about a mind that is uncontaminated? You and I are not newborn, we have been contaminated by society, by Hinduism, by education, by the family, by society, by newspapers. How do we break through the contamination? Do I say it is part of my existence and accept it? What do I do, sir? Here is a problem—that our minds are contaminated. For the older ones it is more difficult to break through. You are comparatively young and the problem is to uncontaminate the mind; how is it to be done?

Either it is possible, or it is not possible. Now how is one to discover whether it is or not? I would like you to jump into it.

Do you know what is meant by the word "denial"? What

does it mean to deny the past, to deny being a Hindu? What do you mean by that word "deny"? Have you ever denied anything? There is a true denial and a false denial. The denial with a motive is a false denial. The denial with a purpose, the denial with an intention, with an eye on the future, is not a denial. If I deny something in order to get something more, it is not denial. But there is a denial which has no motive. When I deny and do not know what is in store for me in the future, that is true denial. I deny being a Hindu, I deny belonging to any organisation, I deny any particular creed and in that very denial I make myself completely insecure. Do you know such a denial, and have you ever denied anything? Can you deny the past that way—deny, not knowing what is in the future? Can you deny the known?

Teacher: When I deny something—say Hinduism, there is a simultaneous understanding of what Hinduism is.

Krishnamurti: What we were discussing is the bringing about of a new mind and if it is possible. A mind that is contaminated cannot be a new mind. So we are talking of de-contamination, and whether that is possible. And in relation to that I began by asking what you mean by denial, because I think denial has a great deal to do with it. Denial has to do with a new mind. If I deny cleanly, without roots, without motive, it is real denial. Now is that possible? You see, if I do not completely deny society in which is involved politics, economics, social relationships, ambition, greed—if I do not deny all that completely, it is impossible to find out what it is to have a new mind. Therefore, the first breaking of the foundation is the denial of the things I have known. Is that possible?

Obviously, drugs will not bring about a new mind; nothing will bring it about except a total denial of the past. Is it possible? What do you say? And if I have felt the perfume, the sight, the taste of such denial, how do I help to convey it to a student? He must have in abundance the known—mathematics, geography, history—and yet be abundantly free of the known, remorselessly free of it.

Teacher: Sir, all sensations leave a residue, a disturbance which lead to various kinds of conflict and other forms of mental activity. The traditional approach of all religions is to deny this sensation by discipline and denial. But in what you say there seems to be a heightened receptivity to these sensations so that you see the sensations without distortion or residue.

Krishnamurti: That is the issue. Sensitivity and sensation are two different things. A mind that is a slave to thought, sensation, feeling, is a residual mind. It enjoys the residue, it enjoys thinking about the pleasurable world and each thought leaves a mark, which is the residue. Each thought of a certain pleasure you have had, leaves a mark which makes for insensitivity. It obviously dulls the mind and discipline, control and suppression further dull the mind. I am saying that sensitivity is not sensation, that sensitivity implies no mark, no residue. So what is the question?

Teacher: Is the denial of which you are speaking different from a denial which is the restriction of sensation?

Krishnamurti: How do you see those flowers, see the beauty of them, be completely sensitive to them so that there is no residue, no memory of them, so that when you see them again an hour later you see a new flower? That is not possible if you see as a sensation and that sensation is associated with flowers, with pleasure. The traditional way is to shut out what is pleasurable because such associations awaken other forms of pleasure and so you discipline yourself not to look. To cut association with a surgical knife is immature. So how is the mind, how are the eyes, to see the tremendous colour and yet have it leave no mark?

I am not asking for a method. How does that state come into being? Otherwise we cannot be sensitive. It is like a photographic plate which receives impressions and is self-renewing. It is exposed, and yet becomes negative for the next impression. So all the time, it is self-cleansing of every pleasure. Is that possible or are we playing with words and not with facts?

The fact which I see clearly is that any residual sensitivity, sensation, dulls the mind. I deny that fact, but I do not know what it is to be so extraordinarily sensitive that experience leaves no mark and yet to see the flower with fullness, with tremendous intensity. I see as an undeniable fact that every sensation, every feeling, every thought, leaves a mark, shapes the mind, and that such marks cannot possibly bring about a new mind. I see that to have a mind with marks is death, so I deny death. But I do not know the other. I also see that a good mind is sensitive without the residue of experience. It experiences, but the experience leaves no mark from which it draws further experiences, further conclusions, further death.

The one I deny and the other I do not know. How is this transition from the denial of the known to the unknown to come into being?

How does one deny? Does one deny the known, not in great dramatic incidents but in little incidents? Do I deny when I am shaving and I remember the lovely time I had in Switzerland? Does one deny the remembrance of a pleasant time? Does one grow aware of it, and deny it? That is not dramatic, it is not spectacular, nobody knows about it. Still this constant denial of little things, the little wipings, the little rubbings off, not just one great big wiping away, is essential. It is essential to deny thought as remembrance, pleasant or unpleasant, every minute of the day as it arises. One is doing it not for any motive, not in order to enter into the extraordinary state of the unknown. You live in Rishi Valley and think of Bombay or Rome. This creates a conflict, makes the mind dull, a divided thing. Can you see this and wipe it away? Can you keep on wiping away not because you want to enter into the unknown? You can never know what the unknown is because the moment you recognise it as the unknown you are back in the known.

The process of recognition is a process of the continued known. As I do not know what the unknown is I can only do this one thing, keep on wiping thought away as it arises.

You see that flower, feel it, see the beauty, the intensity, the extraordinary brilliance of it. Then you go to the room in which you live, which is not well proportioned, which is ugly. You live in the room but you have a certain sense of beauty and you begin to think of the flower and you pick up the thought as it arises and you wipe it away. Now from what depth do you wipe, from what depth do you deny the flower, your wife, your gods, your economic life? You have to live with your wife, your children, with this ugly monstrous society. You cannot withdraw from life. But when you deny totally thought, sorrow, pleasure, your relationship is different and so there must be a total denial, not a partial denial, not a keeping of the things which you like and a denying of the things which you do not like.

Now, how do you translate what you have understood to the student?

Teacher: You have said that in teaching and learning, the situation is one of intensity where you do not say "I am teaching you something". Now this constant wiping away of the marks of thought, has it something to do with the intensity of the teaching-learning situation?

Krishnamurti: Obviously. You see, I feel that teaching and learning are both the same. What is taking place here? I am not teaching you—I am not your teacher or authority, I am merely exploring and conveying my exploration to you. You can take it or leave it. The position is the same with regard to students.

Teacher: What is the teacher then to do?

Krishnamurti: You can only find out when you are constantly denying. Have you ever tried it? It is as if you cannot sleep for a single minute during the day time.

Teacher: It not only needs energy, sir, but also releases a lot of energy.

Krishnamurti: But first you must have the energy to deny.

5 / On Competition

We have been talking of establishing a right communication between ourselves and the student, and in the state of communion to bring about a different atmosphere or climate, in which the student begins to learn. I do not know if you have noticed that as frivolity is contagious so is seriousness. It is a seriousness that does not arise because of a heavy face or a heavy heart but a seriousness which comes into being when we are in a state of relationship, communion.

I think learning can exist only in that state of communion between the teacher and the student, as between you and me —not that I am your teacher. You know what the word "communion" means: to communicate, to be in touch, to transmit a certain feeling, to share it, not only at the verbal level but also at an intellectual level and also to feel much more deeply, subtly. I think the word "communion" means all that, and in that state, at all levels, in that atmosphere, in that sense of togetherness, is it not possible for both the teacher and the student to learn? I think that is the only state in which to learn, not when you sit on a pedestal and pour information down the throat of the student. Could we establish that communion, not only with the speaker but with trees, with nature, with the world, with the early morning when we get up, a sense of communion in which we learn?

This morning could we discuss something which I feel not only the professional teacher but the human being should consider, because what we are to discuss has a great deal of significance in life? The whole of civilization, not only in India but in the rest of the world, is geared to competition, to success, to achievement. The ambitious man seems to be the respected entity—the ambitious man, the aggressive man who wants to succeed, to intrigue, to pull strings and so get to the top of the heap. There is everlasting competition not only in the class room of a school but also in daily life, in the attitude of the clerk who feels he must become the manager and the manager the director and the director the board president and so on. This is the established pattern of existence in modern civilization. You see everywhere that man is after success and it is he who is respected, politically at least, and the same attitude exists in the school. You tell the student he is not as good, not as intelligent as another student. You coax the child, goad him, encourage him to compete, to succeed, to arrive at a certain intellectual level. You are worshippers of labels.

So you have an inborn attitude, which is essentially competitive and aggressive. This is so not only in economic and social life but also in religious life. There is this everlasting struggle to climb, to compete, to compare at all the levels of our being. Do you question this background of the superior and the inferior or do you accept it as inevitable and carry on? And will this bring about real learning? Is this natural to life? Natural not in the primitive sense of that word but is this a cultured life? Would you bring up your child this way? Do you think it is the right way of existence? I know it is the accepted pattern, but is it the true way? First of all, what does this competition, this comparison, do to the mind? Do you think you learn through competition? Let us examine this. You know that it is the established pattern at all levels of our being, at all stages of our existence, to compare, to have goals, to achieve. This is the whole structure of human existence.

When you see two pictures on the wall, your attitude is that if the name of the painter is well known, whatever he paints is excellent. But the man whose name is not known, his picture is inferior. This happens all the time. Is that right? Will that attitude bring comprehension, will that help us to learn? Not that I must not have the capacity to discriminate, but will comparison help the mind to understand, to learn? Is comparison a state of mind in which one learns?

How will you proceed to help the student if both you and the student have this attitude of competition, of comparison?

Let us make this very simple. What does this competition do to the mind? What happens to the mind that is always comparing, achieving success, worshipping success?

Teacher: It is tiring itself.

Krishnamurti: You are still watching the effects, the results, but you are not watching the mind itself. You are not watching the nature of the mind itself which is doing this, the mind which is in movement, which is in a state of competition. Please look at the mind itself which is doing these things.

Teacher: If the mind is going to measure success by achievement, when it does not achieve, there is frustration.

Krishnamurti: You are still dealing with results. I want to tackle the mind. Perhaps analogies are tiring. The seed of an oak can never become the pine tree. You say: "I do not know what seed I am but I want to become a pine, or an ash, or the oak". We do not know the seed or the state of the mind itself, but concern ourselves with what it should be.

Let us experience the thing rather than verbalise it. We compete, worship success, because we feel that if we did not compete, we would stagnate. That is merely a speculative response, it is not an actual fact. You do not know what would happen. When you see what you are, whatever it is, then you begin to learn. Water is water in all circumstances whether it is in the river or in a single drink. At present we have no foundation from which to learn. What we are doing is merely adding. The additive process is what we call learning. It is not learning.

It is only the mind that is in a state in which it is not comparing, when it has understood the absurdity of comparing, that it can establish a foundation from which it can start to learn in the true sense of the word.

If there is such a foundation in which there is no wandering, no longing, it is a solid foundation and on that you can build. The building is the structure of learning and from that learning there is action and never conformity, and therefore never a sense of fear, never a sense of frustration.

Can you help the student to learn in that manner? For the student to learn, you must differentiate totally between the process of addition and learning. Then, you are creating a real human being, not a machine. If you do not see that, how are you going to help the student? Can you wipe away all competition with one sweep, which means can you wipe away the so-called structure of a society?

You are teachers; a new generation is coming into your hands. Do you want them to continue in the same way? If you feel that this society in which we have grown up is a rotten thing, how will you help the student to create a new quality of mind in which the monstrosity of competition has no part? What are the steps you will take, day after day, to see that the child is not drowned, swallowed up by society? What will you do, step by step, to help him?

Teacher: The child should not be brought up with luxuries.

Krishnamurti: What is wrong with luxuries? He may wear clean clothes, he may sit in a chair, have good food. To me it is luxury, to you it is not. What has luxury to do with this? You are laying down the law, the ideal of "luxury".

Talk to the child not once a week, talk to him about it all the time, because he is being conditioned to compete. How will you help him not to be caught in the vicious circle of competition?

Teacher: By making him see that he should not be afraid and that as an individual he is unique and has a contribution to make.

Krishnamurti: If an individual realizes he is unique, so unique that there is no other like him, is he unique factually? He comes with all the prejudices of his parents. Where is the uniqueness in that poor child? You have to strip him of all his conditioning and can you strip him of it? Is it not your function as a teacher to do that? It is your responsibility. You have to see it, to see that it is true; and you have to feel it so that you will transmit it. But the boy may not feel it is so urgent. How will you commune with the child so that he learns? How will you teach him or help him to learn without the spirit of competition?

Teacher: I am not able to feel for the child unless the feeling is inside me, and when it is not there I feel I have already destroyed the child.

Krishnamurti: I will tell you. Every case has its own lesson. You do not feel it because you yourself are competing. Are you not competing for money, position, prestige? As long as you do not feel strongly about this, what will you do? You cannot wait till you completely understand. So what will you do? Do not give the student marks but keep a record for yourself to see how he is behaving, how he is learning and the stage of his knowledge and so on, but do not goad him and help him to compete.

Let us go over what we have discussed. Real learning comes about when the competitive spirit has ceased. The competitive spirit is merely an additive process which is not learning at all. We want the child to learn and not merely add knowledge to himself like a machine. To help the child to learn basically and fundamentally he must cease to compete, with all its implications. Now, one of the ways to do this is to see the truth of not comparing. Now, how will you help the child not to be competitive?

Teacher: As I teach mathematics I think of the ways I can present the subject matter so that it will be interesting. So many things operate in relationship when a thing like this is presented, and how do we communicate them? It is a very vast thing, so we can only say it in parts.

Krishnamurti: You are not meeting the point. When I say: "What will you do?" I mean not only in terms of action but also in terms of feeling. They are not two different things, the feeling and the action. I see very clearly that competitiveness is destructive not only in the class-room but right through life. Here is a young child; I want to help him to understand. How am I to proceed? I can talk to him and say, "Look at what is happening in life. There is misery, conflict." Talk to him so that you do not create condemnation, you do not create reaction. Look at the picture. See it very clearly as you would see London or Bombay on the map. Help the student to see very clearly, that is the first job. Convey to him the urgency of the feeling. Do not try to convince him, influence him, do not talk to him in terms of condemnation, in terms of agreement, persuasion. Show him the fact. Establish the fact. Then you are dealing with him entirely factually, scientifically, not romantically, sentimentally or emotionally. You have established between him and you right relationship. You are dealing with facts and you have established a relationship between you of mutual understanding of the fact, the corruptive fact of competition. Then he and you sit down and say "What are we going to do actually, in action?"

Translation of the feeling of communion depends entirely on the intensity of this feeling. Now, you have established the feeling, the truth, the fact, that competition is deadly, but you have not communicated this fact to the child. That is the first thing to do.

6 / On Fear

Krishnamurti: How would you, as an educator, tackle the problem of the eradication of fear in the student? Can you set about it as you would set about teaching mathematics? First, you must understand fear for yourself before you can help another. You have to understand the implication of fear, how fear comes about. Just as you know Hindi or some other subject, you have to know something of fear. Society is doing everything to inculcate fear by laying down standards, religious ideals, class distinctions, ideas of success, the sense of the inferior and the superior, the rich man and the poor man. Society is doing everything possible to breed distorted values.

The question is not only for the teacher to go deeply into fear but also to see that fear is not transmitted and for the student to be able to recognize the causes that breed fear. As teachers, would this not be a problem to you? We have very little love in our lives, not only to receive but to give; love not in any mystical sense but the actual feeling of love, pity, compassion, generosity, an action which does not emanate from a centre. And as you have very little love, what would you do with the student, how would you help him to have this flame?

Does religion mean anything to you? Not ceremonies, but the religious feeling, the religious benediction, the sacredness of something? Religion, fear, love—are they not very interrelated? You cannot understand the one without the other. There is fear, there is this appalling dearth of love—I mean the passion of it, the intensity of it—and then there is this feeling of benediction which is not mere recompense, which is not a reward for righteous action, which has nothing to do with religious organisations.

Do you walk in the evening and have you noticed those villagers crossing the fields? How beautiful it all is? And the villager is totally unconscious of the beauty of the land, of the hills, of the water. For the villager returning to his unhealthy home there is nothing. There is fear, there is the immense problem of love and the feeling of sympathy when you see the poor villager go by. Don't you feel a tremendous surging in yourself, a despair at the colossal misery of it all? What can one do? There is the ability to receive and to give, to feel, and to have generosity, kindness, humility. What does it mean to you? How do you awaken this thing in yourself or awaken it in another? Can there be an approach that is not an isolated critical comprehension but an understanding that is total—of fear, love, the religious feeling?

Now how am I to approach the problem? Am I to take

each problem one by one, to take fear, look at it, and then study love? How am I to capture the whole thing? If you have the feeling of a sound, you have the feeling of a song and if you have a feeling for the silence between sounds you have the delight of the movement of a song. Song is not just the word, just the sound, it is the peculiar combination of the sound, the silence and the continuation of the sound. To understand music surely there must be comprehension of the whole thing. And in the same way, is fear an isolated problem which has to be comprehended by itself and love by itself and the religious feeling by itself, or is there an approach to the whole, a total thing?

Have you ever watched a rain drop? The rain drop contains the whole of the rain, the whole of the river, the whole of the ocean. That drop makes the river, makes the ravines, excavates the Grand Canyon, becomes a vibrant thundering waterfall. In the same way can my mind look at fear, love, religion, god, as a movement, rather than as an isolated introspection, an analytical examination, a dissection?

Teacher: What is the relationship between fear and love?

Krishnamurti: If I am afraid, how can I have sympathy for anybody? An ambitious man does not know about the earth and the brotherhood of man. An ambitious man knows no love. Can a man who is afraid of death, of what his neighbours might say, of his wife, security, job, have sympathy? The one excludes the other.

Teacher: We operate only in parts, we try through parts to apprehend the whole.

Krishnamurti: What will transform fear?

Teacher: Understanding.

Krishnamurti: What brings the transformation and who is to transform? I have observed my mind which says, "I am afraid" and I want to get at what my mind is trying to do. What is effort and who is the maker of effort? Unless one goes into it very deeply, the mere saying "I must get rid of fear" has very little meaning.

There is fear, there is love, and this feeling of immensity. I can analyse fear step by step. I can go into the causes of fear, the effects of fear, I can go into why I am afraid, and who is the maker of effort and whether the maker of effort is different from the thing which is making effort. And I can enquire into whether there is a mind which can observe effort, the maker of effort and the thing upon which he is making an effort, not only objectively but inwardly. At the end of it all, there is still lurking fear. I can go very analytically into this question of religion, dogma, belief, superstition but at the end of this analysis I am still where I am. I have learned the techniques of analysis and at the end of it, my mind is so sharp that it can follow every movement of fear. But fear still lurks.

Now what is the nature of the mind that takes in the whole, digests it at one sweep and throws out what is not worthwhile?

There must be an approach which will give one a total comprehension, a total feeling with which one can approach each problem. Can I capture the whole meaning of something, of love, fear, religion, that extraordinary feeling of immensity, of beauty and then approach each problem individually? You have seen trees. Do you take in the whole tree or do you merely look at the branch and the leaves and the flower? Do you see the whole tree inside you? After all, a tree is the root, the branch, the flower, the fruit, the sap, the whole of the tree. Can you grasp the feeling, the significance, the beauty of the whole tree and then look at the branch? Such an observation will have tremendous significance.

When you look at a tree next time, see the shape of it, the symmetry of it, the depth, the feeling, the beauty, the quality of the whole thing. I am talking of the feeling of the whole. In the same way you have a body: you have feelings, emotions; there is the mind, there are memories—the conscious and unconscious traditions, the centuries of accumulated impressions, the family name—can you feel the whole of that? If you do not feel the whole of that but merely dissect your emotions, it is immature. Can you feel within yourself this whole thing and with that feeling of the whole being, attack fear?

Fear is an immense problem. Can you approach it with an immensity to meet an immensity?

Teacher: It is not always possible, sir, we often get lost in our immediate problems.

Krishnamurti: But once you have the feeling of this immensity, life has a different colouration, it has a different quality.

Teacher: You are only conscious of this immensity at times.

Krishnamurti: I do not think you have ever thought of it, have you?

Teacher: Yes, I have, once in a way, by detaching myself from the immediate problem and looking at it.

Krishnamurti: I do not mean that. I mean to have the feeling of all time, not today, tomorrow, the day after day, but the feeling of all time. To think in terms of man, the world, the universe is an extraordinary feeling. And with that feeling can one approach the particular problem? Otherwise we are going to land in an intellectual or emotional chaos.

What is the difficulty in this? Is it the incapacity, the narrowness of the mind, the immediate occupation, the immediate concern for the child, the husband, the wife which so takes up your time that you have no time to think of it? Take the word, "immediate". There is no immediate, it is an endless thing. You make it into an immediate problem; that problem is the result of a thousand yesterdays and a thousand tomorrows. There is no immediacy. There is fear, love and man's urge for the immense. Can you capture some of the quality of the feeling and say, "Let me look at fear"?

What significance has fear, and how will you proceed to help the student? You should prepare the student for the whole of life, and life is an extraordinarily vast thing. And when you use the word "life" it is all the oceans and the mountains and the trees and all of human aspirations, human miseries, despairs, struggles, the immensity of it all. Can you help the student to apprehend that immensity of life? Must you not help the student to have this feeling?

Do any of you meditate? Not only to sit still, not only to examine the ways of the mind but also to invite the conscious and the unconscious and to push further into silence and see what happens further and further. If you do not do this, are you not missing a lot in life?

Meditation is a form of self-recollected awareness, a form of discovery, a form of cutting loose from tradition, from ideas, conclusions, a sense of being completely alone, which is death. With that sense of the total, can you meet the immediate?

Let us become a little more practical. How do we set about to help the student actually to be free from fear?

Teacher: I would see that my relationship with the student is friendly. It would be stupid to discuss fear if I were not friendly with him. I would create situations, both practical and intellectual, where he would understand what fear actually means, intellectually explain the causes and effects of fear because the mind needs to be sharpened, and I would see if I could make him experience this wholeness of outlook and feeling.

Krishnamurti: Be factual. In the class, how will you teach? How will you help the student to understand? There is a gap between the child and the total feeling, how would you lead up to that?

Teacher: It should be possible to awaken in him a curiosity which is of a subtle type. The next thing I would like to do with him is to get him to appreciate quality in work, in playing a game, in mathematics or other subjects. I would find out what his interests were, how he reacted, and if I were able to progress further, I would see whether something more happened between me and the student.

Krishnamurti: You have done the obvious things which are necessary. You would talk to him, you would show him how fear comes into being and all that. What next? Factually how will you help the student to be free from fear? I think that is the real issue. When there is an opportunity, would you be in a meditative, reflective self-recollected state which might help the student to see clearly what fear is? You see that is the necessary thing, but you leave that thing hanging.

What would you actually do? What would you do factually?

Teacher: Meditation would help the mind to deal with the situation.

Krishnamurti: I may have a feeling for all this. Now how am I to translate it into action? What am I to do with those dozen children?

Teacher: The feeling will translate itself. It is a link of love with the children which will help.

Krishnamurti: First have affection, then use every occasion to help the student to be free from fear, explain to him the causes of fear and use every incident to show how he is afraid. In the class, in the very teaching of history, mathematics, talk to him about it. But what next? Proceed.

Teacher: In doing all this I am also watchful to see that what I am doing to him is not also being undone.

Krishnamurti: What is the total effect on the child of what you have said, the fact of your affection, your explanations? Is it not making him turn inward, and what does that do?

Teacher: It helps him face some immediate problems.

Krishnamurti: You have helped the student to look at himself, you have helped him to be aware of this fear and to turn inward in the sense that he feels more conscious of the fear. You have to balance it by something else.

Teacher: Do you mean, sir, that this process of internal introspection is likely to lead to some complications in the child?

Krishnamurti: It is bound to lead to a kind of self-conscious feeling. "Am I doing the right thing or the wrong thing?" There would be nervousness or self importance, or the showing off in "How fearless I am!" How will you balance that? Think it out, use your mind very carefully. At this stage I think the problem again requires a different kind of approach. Otherwise you will be helping the child by concentrated attention to become self-conscious, self-assertive, arrogant, and with an authoritarian outlook.

Teacher: There should be an opportunity for the child to be sensitive to other things which are not within.

Krishnamurti: It appears to me, you will unconsciously strengthen egotism, a sense of self-importance, a sense of being assertive, aggressive, rude.

You have so far dealt with the movement of the mind. The tide is moving in, the tide also moves out. If it remains inward it is like the backwaters of a bay, but if the tide has a movement inward, then it has to have an outward movement. You have dealt so far only with an inward movement. How will you help the student to move out?

Teacher: When you spoke of the outward movement, I felt I was not looking from the point of the whole but from the development of the partial movement.

Krishnamurti: If I had not kept on pushing and therefore made you realize it was only a partial answer, you would not have moved. You only talk of the inner movement but it is a movement of the tide both inward and outward. It is a movement you have treated in one direction and you do not know how to treat the inner and the outer as one movement.

Teacher: Is it not possible right from the beginning to move both inward and outward?

Krishnamurti: What is the outward movement that is going to give the balance?

Teacher: Not only the balance, but a sense of humility that comes now and then.

Krishnamurti: There are hills, trees, the river, the sands. That is the outward movement. The perception, the seeing, that is the outward movement. Nature has provided you with the beauty of all this, the rivers, trees, the arid land. So there has to be movement both outward and inward, the everlasting movement.

7 / On Teaching and Learning

Teacher: We realize that we cannot see a fact unless the mind is empty of thought. But even if it is empty for a while, thought seems to arise again. How do we end thought? Can we discuss this?

Krishnamurti: I wonder if all of us understand the importance of the role of thinking? Is thought important, and at what level is it important? What is thinking? What makes us think? Where is thought important and where is it not important, and how do you answer that question? And what is the machinery that is set going when a question is asked?

Is thinking merely the habitual response to a habitual pattern? You live here in this school in a certain groove, with certain patterns of thoughts, habits, feelings. You live, you function in those habits, patterns and systems, and the functioning of the brain, thought is very limited. And when you go out of the valley you live in a little wider field. You have certain grooves of action and you follow them. It is all a mechanical process really, but in that pattern of mechanical activity there are certain variations. You modify, change, but always in that pattern, wherever you are, whatever position you may have—minister, governor or doctor, or professor— it is always a groove with varying changes and modifications. You function in patterns. I am not saying it is right or wrong, I am just examining it. You have beliefs but they are in the background and you go on with your daily activities, with your envy, greed, jealousy. Whenever your beliefs are questioned you get irritated but you go on. Children are being educated to think, to form grooves of habits and to function in those habits for the rest of their lives. They are going to get jobs, they are going to be engineers, doctors, and for the rest of their lives, the pattern will be set. Any deviation from that is what is disturbing. That disturbance is lessened through marriage, responsibility, children; and so gradually the mould is set. And all thinking is between what is convenient, what is not convenient, what is beneficial, what is worthwhile—it is always within that field.

Teacher: That is not thinking, sir, it is a repetition.

Krishnamurti: But that is how we live, that is our life. That is all we want. Everything is repetition and the mind gets duller and more stupid. Is that not a fact, sir? We do not want to be disturbed, we do not want to shatter the pattern.

What makes us shatter the pattern or break through the pattern? And is it possible not to fall into a groove? But why should I end the making of patterns? I begin to think about ending them when the pattern does not satisfy me, when the pattern is no longer useful to me or when there are in the pattern certain incidents like death, the husband leaving the wife, or losing a job. In the breaking of that particular pattern there is a disturbance called sorrow and I move away from that into another pattern. I move from pattern to pattern, from one framework into which circumstances, environment, family, education have put me, to another. The disturbance makes me question a little, but I immediately fall into another groove and there I settle. That is what most people want, what their parents want, what society wants. Where does this idea of ending thought come in?

Teacher: Sir, there are times when one is discontented with the whole pattern and everything in it.

Krishnamurti: What makes us see the futility of this pattern? When do I see it and what makes me see it? A pattern is set if there is a motive. If I break from this pattern with a motive, the motive will mould the new pattern.

Now, what makes me change, what makes me do something without a motive?

Teacher: It is very difficult to be free from motive.

Krishnamurti: Who tells you to be free? If it is difficult, why bother about breaking the pattern? Be satisfied with a motive and continue with it, why bother if it is difficult?

Teacher: It leads me nowhere, sir.

Krishnamurti: But if it led anywhere, would you pursue it?

Teacher: Which means there is a motive again.

Krishnamurti: What makes you break through and give up the motive? What do you mean by motive? You teach here because you get some money, that is a motive. You like some-body because he can give you a position or you love god because you hate life. Your life is miserable, and love of god is the escape from that. These are all motives.

Now, what makes a mind, a human being, live without a motive? If you can pursue that and go into it, I am sure you will find the answer to your question.

Teacher: The question, "Do I know my motives?" seems to come before the question "Do I do something without a motive?"

Krishnamurti: Do we know our motives? Why do I teach, why do I hold on to a husband, wife? Do I know my motives, and how do I find out? And if I do find out, what is wrong with having motives. I love somebody because I like to be with that somebody physically, sexually, as a companion, what is wrong with that?

Teacher: When I teach because I must have money, motive is not a hindrance. I must have money, so I must take to some profession, and I take to teaching.

Krishnamurti: First of all, do we know our motives, not only the conscious but the unconscious motives, the hidden mo-tives? Do we do anything in our lives without a motive? To do something without a motive is love of what one is doing, and in that process thinking is not mechanical; then the brain is in a state of constant learning, not opinionated, not moving from knowledge to knowledge. It is a mind that moves from fact to fact. Therefore, such a mind is capable of ending and coming to something it does not know, which is freedom from the known.

You asked at the beginning: "How do we end thought?"

I said: "What for?" We do not even know what thinking is, we do not know how to think. We think in terms of patterns. So, unless we have investigated or understood all that, we cannot possibly ask that question: "How do we end thought?"

Teacher: How can we enquire into thinking and how to think?

Krishnamurti: Not only enquire into how to think but also into what is thinking. Can I, as a human being, as an individual, find out what is the way of my thinking? Is it mechanical, is it free? Do I know it as it is operating in me?

To end thought I have first to go into the mechanism of thinking. I have to understand thought completely, deep down in me. I have to examine every thought, without letting one thought escape without being fully understood, so that the brain, the mind, the whole being becomes very attentive. The moment I pursue every thought to the root, to the end completely, I will see that thought ends by itself. I do not have to do anything about it because thought is memory. Memory is the mark of experience and as long as experience is not fully, completely, totally understood, it leaves a mark. The moment I have experienced completely, the experience leaves no mark. So, if we go into every thought and see where the mark is and remain with that mark, as a fact—then that fact will open and that fact will end that particular process of thinking, so that every thought, every feeling is understood. So the brain and the mind are being freed from a mass of memories. That requires tremendous attention, not attention only to the trees and birds but inward attention to see that every thought is understood.

Teacher: That seems to be a vicious circle. The mind is

involved in getting rid of a pattern of thinking and in order to understand the process of thinking it needs a certain sensitivity which the mind does not have.

Krishnamurti: Take a thought, any kind of thought. Go into it. See why you have such a thought, what is involved in it, understand it, do not leave it till you have completely unearthed all the roots of it.

Teacher: That can only be done if the instrument which is doing it, is sensitive.

Krishnamurti: As you go into one particular thought you are beginning to understand the instrument which is examining that thought. Then what is important is not the thought but the observer who is examining the thought. And the observer is the thought which says: "I do not like that thought, I like this thought." So you attack the core of thought and not just the symptoms. And as you are a teacher, how will you create this or bring about this attentive observation, this examination without any judgement, in a student?

If I may ask: How do you teach? What is the environment, the condition, the atmosphere, in which teaching and learning are possible? You teach, say, history, and the student learns. What is the atmosphere, the environment, the quality in the room in which teaching and learning are taking place?

Teacher: There is a special atmosphere when the teacher and the student are both attending.

Krishnamurti: I do not want to use the word "attention". If you learn anything from the teacher, what is the nature of that communication, of receiving and learning? For a flower to grow it must have rain, do you understand?

Teacher: Could we approach it negatively?

Krishnamurti: In any way you like. I am asking you to teach science. What is the atmosphere in the room where you teach science? Where the teacher and the student are learning, teaching? What is the quality necessary, what is the atmosphere, the smell, the perfume?

Teacher: A quiet and calm environment.

Krishnamurti: You are idealistic and I am not. I have not one ideal inside me, I just want to know the fact. You are moving away from the fact, that is what I object to. When you teach and they learn, in the class room, what is the atmosphere? The atmosphere is the fact.

Teacher: Friendliness between the teacher and the student.

Krishnamurti: You are not facing the fact. You teach and you also know and when the student is to learn, there must be a certain quality, and I am asking what is that quality? Have you actually experienced the quality where this communication is mutual, where the learning is the teaching?

Teacher: In the beginning I thought that when I teach, I am handing over some facts to the students, but now I understand that when I am teaching there is also a learning. This happens at rare moments when there is exploration, when both the teacher and the student are exploring together.

Krishnamurti: What is the state when that exploration together takes place? What is the atmosphere, the relationship? What is the word you would use to express that state in which communication is possible?

Teacher: Curiosity.

Krishnamurti: What do you teach?

Teacher: Hindi.

Krishnamurti: The children are anxious to know and you are anxious to teach. Now, what atmosphere does it create? What takes place?

Teacher: The children listen to me.

Krishnamurti: You say children listen to you. You want to tell them something. What has happened, I wish you would examine this.

Teacher: There is a state of alertness.

Krishnamurti: I want to go a little bit more into the matter. The moment you say it is alertness you have already put it in a framework. I am trying to prevent you and myself from defining it.

Teacher: When the object is there, the object of learning and teaching, both operate; from this there is a fluidity, a movement; and temporarily, this state is slightly different from the other states I know.

Krishnamurti: There is attention when the teacher and the taught, both have a drive to learn and to teach. You have to create a feeling, an atmosphere, in the room. Just now we have created an atmosphere—because I want to find out and you want to find out. Is it possible to maintain this atmosphere, in which alone teaching and learning are possible?

We started by asking how to communicate this sense of enquiry into thinking, into motive, to the student. I asked you, how do you teach, that is, how do you convey anything? And I asked what takes place when you actually teach. What is the atmosphere when you are teaching? Is it a slack atmosphere or a tense atmosphere? Now, if you have not examined your thinking, the mechanism of thinking, to convey the sense of enquiry to the student is impossible. But if you have done it in yourself, you are bound to create the atmosphere. And I feel that atmosphere, that attention, is the essential quality of teaching and learning.

Teacher: You have said that definition of a fact is something quite different from the experiencing of that fact. Now in all this there seems to be a gap between the definition and the actual doing of something. You also asked: Have you ever done something for its own sake because you love it? How does one, without examining one's motives, without all these ramifications, get to the heart of something?

Krishnamurti: That is just what I was trying to get at. To see something totally is the ending of time or the comprehending of it. Can one see if there is a motive in teaching and learning at any level? Life is a constant process of teaching and learning: To teach and to learn is not possible if there is a motive, and when we have a motive the state of teaching and learning is not possible. Now, watch this carefully: In the very nature of teaching and learning there is humility. You are the teacher and you are the taught. So there is no pupil and no teacher, no *guru* and no *sishya;* there is only teaching and learning, which is going on in me. I am learning and I am also teaching myself; the whole process is one. That is important. That gives vitality, a sense of depth, and that is prevented if I have a motive. As teaching-learning is important, everything else becomes secondary and therefore, motive disappears. What is important drives away the unimportant. Therefore it is finished: I do not have to examine my motives day after day.

Teacher: It is not very clear to me, sir.

Krishnamurti: First of all, life is a process of learning. It is not saying "I have learned" and a settling back. Life is a process of learning and I cannot learn if there is a motive. If that is very clear, that life is a process of learning, then motive has no place. Motive has a place when you are using learning to get something. So the essential fact drives away all the unessential trivialities, in which motive is included.

Teacher: Should there be a concern for the essential, as a fact?

Krishnamurti: But the fact is the essential. Life is the essential. Life is "what is". Otherwise it is not life. If motive is not, "what is" is. If you understand the fact of sorrow, the "other" comes into being. You cannot come to the "other" without understanding motive, the unessential.

Teacher: So there cannot be concern for the essential.

Krishnamurti: Understand the fact, which is important, and go into it. If you are ambitious, be completely ambitious. Let there be no double thinking. Be either ambitious or see the fact of ambition. Both are facts, and when you examine one fact, go into it completely. If you go into the fact completely, the fact will begin to show what is involved in ambition. The fact of ambition will begin to unravel itself and then there is no ambition.

Most religious people have invented theories about facts. But they do not understand "the fact". Having established a theory they hope it will ward off the actual fact; it cannot. So do not try to establish any essential fact. See how you slip into wrong action. There is no essential fact, there is only fact—you see the point? And one fact does not conform to another fact. The moment it is conforming, it is not a fact. If you look at the fact with a referent, with what you can get out of that fact, then you will never see the fact. To look at the fact is the only thing that matters. There is no fact that is superior or inferior, there is only fact. That is the ruthless thing. If I am a lawyer, I am a lawyer. I do not find excuses for it. Seeing that fact, going into it, seeing the motives, the fact and its complexities are revealed, and then you are out of it. But if you say, "I must always speak the truth", that is an ideal. That is a false assumption. So do not move from what you consider the unimportant fact to what you consider the more important fact. There is only fact, not the less or the more. It really does something to you to look at life that way. You banish all illusion, all dissipation of energy of the mind, the brain, at one stroke. The mind then operates in precision without any deception, without hatred, without hypocrisy. The mind then becomes very clear, sharp. That is the way to live.

8 / On the Good Mind

Krishnamurti: I think that most of us have a fairly comprehensive view of what is happening in the world. Looking at the historical processes, the appalling travesty of peace, one must have asked oneself what life is all about. There is the enslaving of whole masses of people; there is corruption and talk of democracy; religions have failed, only superstitions remain. There is the dead weight of tradition, the innumerable *gurus,* soothsayers, monks, astrologers. There is poverty, degradation, the squalor of existence. And there is also a sense of deep despair. So, seeing this immense suffering, what is our answer to it all? There are people who say that what is needed is not a new system or a new philosophy, but rather a new type of leadership, a new type of man who has immense authority not only in the state but in his own idealistic strength. But do we want new leaders? What we need is freedom from leaders.

When we see this vast confusion, economic strangulation and imbalance, and come to Rishi Valley, what is it that a school of this kind can do, and should do? Can we discuss this? Not as an ideal, for ideals of any kind are very detrimental. Ideals prevent us from looking at facts, and it is only a concern with facts and the understanding of facts which releases an energy that is the movement in the right direction. Ideals merely engender various forms of escape. Let us consider all this and see what we can do here in this school.

This is not going from the vast to the ridiculous, for this school is a miniature of what is taking place in the world and, seeing the destructive chaos, misery, suffering, I feel there is only one answer and that is the creation of a new mind. What is essential is a different mind that will look at all problems and find a solution and not create new problems. I think the right kind of education does bring about the good mind, the total development of man, and it seems to me that is the major issue not only in this valley but also in the rest of the world.

How can one bring about a good mind, a mind that sees all these co-relations, not only at the superficial level but a mind that can penetrate inwardly? It seems to me that the problem of education is to see whether it is possible to cultivate an intelligence which is not the result of influence, an intelligence which is not the learning of certain techniques and the earning of a livelihood. They are part of education but surely they are not the only function of education? Now how do you educate a child so that he is able to face life and not merely conform to the established patterns of society, to certain modes of conduct? So that he can go much further, deeper into the whole problem of existence?

I do not know if you have ever considered what a good mind is. Is it a good mind that has the capacity to retain what it reads, and functions from memory? The electronic brain is doing this marvellously. It calculates at astonishing speed some of the most complicated mathematical problems. It functions, I have been told, in the same way as the human brain, doing the desired calculations.

Is a good mind one that repeats, like a gramaphone, what it has been told? That is our education, isn't it? The learning of facts, dates, to repeat them once a year when a boy takes his examination. Can this be called cultivating a good mind? And yet is this not what most of us are doing when we are teaching? So the mere addition to knowledge, which is really the cultivation of memory, is just an additive process. It does not engender a clear, good mind, does it? Negatively, one can see that the mere cultivation of memory does not bring about a good mind although most of our existence is based on this. And yet, one must have memory, one must have a very good memory to remember certain things, to be a good technician. So, at what point does memory interfere with a good mind capable of explanation, investigation and discovery? At what point does memory interfere with real freedom?

I do not know if you have ever considered the man who invented the jet aeroplane. He had first to understand the whole problem of the piston-propeller engine. He had to know it, but after knowing it, he had to put it away in order to discover something new. The specialists, until they really discover something new, merely continue a better and more complicated technique, but if a man is to invent something new he has to let go of the old.

Teacher: Sir, you have said that perception of a fact leads to knowledge in the right direction, whereas ideals lead to escapes. Can you make the statement clearer?

Krishnamurti: How do ideals come into being, and what is the need for ideals? The ideal of what should be, which is away from the fact, limits the mind and makes it static. If a child merely conforms to certain ideals, to the words of certain teachers, to the words of his father, grandfather, uncle and so on, that restrains energy and limits knowledge, does it not? All conformity limits knowledge. If I am an art teacher and I teach children to copy, which is imitation, it does not really help creative perception or expression, does it? Now let us see what happens when there is perception of the fact. I perceive that I am stupid. There is perception, realization, awareness of the fact that I am stupid. That is, I do not give explanations or offer an opinion about my stupidity and thereby escape through explanation. The observation of a fact without justification or condemnation releases tremendous energy. Now is there a release of energy through conformity, through motive, through mere acceptance? And can one function in the framework of that acceptance?

Teacher: Physically, there is.

Krishnamurti: Is physical energy released by conforming? What is the motive behind this extraordinary urge in most of us to conform to a pattern? What is the compulsive urge behind this? Obviously it is the desire to be secure, is it not? Security in your relationship with your wife, with your husband, in the good opinion of the public or a friend. All this indicates the desire not only for economic security but inward mental security or certainty, does it not?

Teacher: The demand for security is the desire to have peace of mind.

Krishnamurti: I need a certain amount of security. I must have a job. If I am uncertain of my next meal I would not be sitting here talking. Does the desire for peace mean that we should have a mind that will never be disturbed? And why should we not be disturbed? What is wrong if we are disturbed? Much of the world is disturbed. Why should we not be disturbed? And, is not the mind which says, "I must not be disturbed", really a dead mind? There can be no state of mind which says, "I am perfectly safe," there can be no mind which is so certain that it will never be disturbed. I think that is the kind of mind most of us want and that is why we conform endlessly. If you had a son, you would want him to conform to the pattern of society because you do not want him to be a revolutionary. So, I am asking what is behind this demand for security, certainty, this hope in which despair is included?

We will come back to it in different way. I am just asking myself, why this urge? Is it fear? I am afraid of not being able to take care of my family and therefore I hold on to my job. I am afraid my wife may not care for me, or my husband may not care for me. I possess property. I am afraid that property may be taken away from me. Behind that threat there is a sense of fear, a desire to be secure.

Teacher: We can only be secure when there is no fear.

Krishnamurti: Wait a minute. Is that possible? You know

what fear is. If most of us were free from all fear, you know what would happen? We would do exactly what we want to do. Fear restrains us, is that not so? But we are asking if a mind that is afraid, anxious, is it ever secure? I may have a good job, I may love my wife or husband, but am I secure when this fear is going on in me? To have no fear, which is an extraordinary state, is to be free of the problem of security. Is it possible for this mind to understand fear and be free from fear? Whatever such a mind does, being free, is right action.

How will you educate a group of children to be fearless? Which does not mean that they can do what they like—but to be free from the sense of all apprehension, anxiety? Will this not release an enormous amount of energy?

How do you set about educating the child? You are afraid and you see that fear is most disturbing. It is the worst form of destruction. How do I educate a boy to be without fear? What is it a teacher can do to translate this into action? Is it to allow the child to think freely? You see the importance of being without fear, because it is death to live in a state of fear. Whether it is conscious or unconscious fear, it troubles your mind. How will you help a child not to be afraid and yet to live with others? He cannot do whatever he likes, he cannot say, "I need not go to the class because I am fearless." Then what makes a child, a student, free? What gives him the deep impression that he is free, not to do what he likes, but free. If a child feels that you are really looking after him, that you care for him, that he is completely at home with you, completely secure with you, that he is not afraid of you, then he respects you and he listens to you because you are looking after him and he has complete confidence in you. He is then at peace with what you tell him. So open the door to him to be without fear. How else will you proceed? First of all you have to establish a relationship with the student, let him know that you really care for him, that he can really feel at home with you and therefore he can be completely at ease and feel secure. It is not a theory, it is not an idea. What will you do if your student fails in an examination? One boy may not be as quick as the other boy and yet he must learn. How will you encourage learning without fear? If you say one boy is better than another, it engenders fear. How will you avoid all this and yet help the child to learn? The child comes from a home where he has been brought up differently. His whole life is geared to achievement, success, and he comes here with all his background of fear and competition. How are you to help him?

Teacher: You can help him learn according to his individual capacity.

Krishnamurti: Let us go slowly. How is it to be done? This school is in your hands. You have to create something out of it. Teaching is a creative thing, it is not merely something you can learn and repeat. How are you going to teach the children in your class for whom you have a feeling of love. Remember they are not interested in learning. They want to have a good time. They want to play cricket, watch birds, and occasionally look at a book. The fact is they want to do the easiest thing. If you leave it to them the more they are secure with you, the more they will exploit you. How will you help them to learn?

You have to find ways to teach them and that is going to release your energy to devise mean of making subjects interesting for the child.

Before you proceed with a child, what is the state of your mind which wants to help the child to learn subjects in which he is not interested?

Teacher: It is the urge to share your learning with the child.

Krishnamurti: I want these children to learn because learning is part of existence and the child can only learn if there is no fear. I must teach the child so that he learns without fear, which means I have to explode with this feeling of wanting to share with that boy. Do you know the state of mind that wants to share with another? That itself seems to be the right feeling. Do you know what that implies? The fact is I know more, the child knows less, and I have a feeling that he must learn, that he must be capable of sharing. We both are learning, which means we are going through an experience together. The child and I are then already in a state of communication. Once I have established the right relationship or communication between myself and the child, he is going to learn because he has confidence in me.

Teacher: The teacher may be very fond of the child, but still the child is not willing to learn, the child is not interested.

Krishnamurti: I question it. When the child has confidence in you, do you think he will not learn any subject you want him to? What we are trying to do is to establish relationship. If that is possible, then will I not convey to the child the importance of learning a subject?

This morning when we began to talk there was no communication between the speaker and the audience. Now we have established some kind of communication and we are trying to work the thing out together. Can we not do the same thing with children?

9 / On the Negative Approach

Krishnamurti: What do you think is right education, not for any particular group of children, the children of the rich or the poor, the children of the village or of the town, but children? How would you bring up a child knowing that walls of destructive nationalism divide people?

Machines are taking over man's labour and man is going to have more leisure. There will be electronic brains, machines which will run by themselves. Man is going to have a great deal of leisure, perhaps not immediately, but in fifty or a hundred years time. Taking into account the advance of technology, growing systematisation, the acceptance of authority and tyranny in the world, what do you consider is the direction of education? What would you consider is the direction of the whole development of man? What is it you want the student to discover for himself?

Are these vain questions? If you consider them seriously what would be your reaction? Machines are going to take over. The perfect teacher, who is really excellent in his subject, can teach a class and his instructions can be recorded through tapes and distributed throughout the world and the ordinary teacher can utilize them and instruct the student. So, the responsibility for good teaching may be taken out of individual hands, though you may need a teacher. You may say that what happens in fifty years is not your immediate problem. But a really good educator must be concerned not only with the immediate but be prepared for the future—future not in the sense of the day after, or a thousand days after tomorrow, but the tendency of this extraordinary development of the mind. I suppose you exist from day to day. The immediate is brutal, tiring and you say: "Why should I bother with what is going to happen?" But if you have a child, if you are a teacher with students, unless you have a total comprehension of all this, you cannot see and understand the meaning of education. What will happen after you educate all these girls and boys? The girls are going to get married and disappear into the vast world. They will be sucked into society. What is the point of educating them? And the boys will get jobs. Why should you educate them to fit into this rotten society? To teach them how to behave, how to be gentle and kind, is that the end of education? Take the total picture of what is happening in the world, not only in India. Seeing this whole picture, comprehending it, what is it you are trying to do?

Unless you have a total response to this whole issue the mere tinkering with it to improve teaching methods has very little meaning. The world is on fire, and being an educated man you must have the right answer to this; being a human being you must have an answer to this, and if you have an answer, a feeling of this totality of evil, then, when you teach mathematics, dancing, singing, it has a significance.

Teacher: Sir, if I do not have this whole feeling towards something, do you think it is likely to come into being when I do something and do it well?

Krishnamurti: I want you to be factual.

Teacher: By being punctual, learning the technique, studying before I teach and doing the thing perfectly, would that help to bring about the quality of total feeling?

Krishnamurti: Would it? It is essential that I be punctual, that I study my subject before I teach—that is understood. And you are asking if that will lead to the total feeling of all this?

Teacher: I feel there is a likelihood—it is not a certainty—when I study something with attention.

Krishnamurti: You have moved away from doing something, from being punctual and all the rest of it, to "attention". What do you mean by attention? I may give a certain meaning to attention and you may not. I will work on mathematics and I will be punctual. I will be very quiet and very tender and affectionate, encourage the student, discourage him from being competitive. Would you call that an attentive mind?

Teacher: I think so, sir. By helping the student not to compete, there is a quality of attention.

Krishnamurti: What does that mean? Not only are you attentive to your subject and to your relationship with the student

but also attentive to nature, to world events and world tendencies, not only to the individual corruptions and individual
aspirations but to the collective. But if you say you are attentive because you go to the class punctually, it has no meaning.

Can you put the question differently? Is it possible to have
this total comprehension without fear? In discussing the possi-
bility of such a comprehension, and discovering it, can we then
turn to the everyday activities and not the other way round?
Now how would you discuss it?

From what do we derive our energy? If we eat a certain
amount of food we have a certain vitality but the vitality is not
the thing that makes us live, function and be conscious. How
do we derive energy, psychological energy, the driving energy? Most people get that energy by having an end in view,
an ego, by maintaining a vision, an ideal, a thing that must be
done, a result. That gives one an astonishing energy. Look at
all the saints and politicians; the wish for success gives them
enormous energy. The man who has an ideal in view and
thinks that it must be established on earth, will walk the earth.
He gets his psychological energy in spite of his body because
that is the thing he must do, because he thinks it is good for
the people and from that he derives an abundant energy. And
when he does not succeed he feels disappointed, depressed,
unhappy, but he covers it up and goes on. Most people derive
energy from wanting a result through the desire to achieve a
position, to fulfil an ambition or an ideal. They get energy with
its accompanying disappointments, frustrations, despair. In
this is the destruction of energy.

If you are interested in god, you want to create the most

beautiful god in the world and you drive yourself, you exhaust yourself, and when the drive becomes a futility, a despair, you become depressed. So you meet a living energy with a negative energy which is depression, sorrow; so there is a contradiction going on.

Teacher: Sir, is energy not destroyed when there is no interest in what one is doing? For example, when a gardener is interested in gardening, there is energy. Is this not real energy and the other one no energy at all?

Krishnamurti: The poor gardener is also depressed if he cannot get what he wants. You are connecting interest with energy and the lack of interest with lack of energy. There are very few of us who are really interested in what we are doing.

Most of us derive our energy from the desire for security, from ideals, from seeking a result, fulfilment of ambition and so on. For most of us that is energy. For the man who goes about doing good, his activity gives him enormous energy and when he does not succeed he is in despair, the two always go together. That energy always brings with it depression, frustration.

In realizing that this form of energy is very destructive, would you not enquire to discover an energy which is not accompanied by depression, by despair, by frustration? Is there such energy? One knows the ordinary energy with its entanglements and one sees that energy which is brought about by seeking a result; and if, seeing it, one pushes it aside, then would that in itself not bring about an enquiry as to whether there is any other form of energy which is not accompanied by despair? That is the problem. Look at that for a little while, consider it, and let us go back to the first question. Seeing this world in flames, the world in utter confusion, and every politician trying to patch it up and every patch having a hole in it—seeing this total state, we must have a total answer. And how do you, as an educator, respond to this? Do you respond with the energy which is destructive or with the energy which is not destructive?

Teacher: What is that energy which has no shadow of destruction in it?

Krishnamurti: Do not ask that question. Never put a positive question. Always put a negative question in order to find a positive answer which is not the response of the opposite.

Now, what is negative thinking? What is this energy which is not destructive? That is a positive question.

What is this total energy? Would it be right for us to describe this total energy which is not destructive, and can I describe it? If I were to describe it, would it not be merely verbal, theoretical to others?

Energy becomes a destructive thing the moment you want to achieve it. The desire to achieve it becomes the end for which you strive and if you do not achieve it, you are in despair. So your question was a wrong question and if one is not very careful, a wrong answer will ensue. So, what should the next question be: "How will you help me to experience this total energy?" If I were able to help you, you would be depending on the helper and the helper may be wrong. So how would you put the question?

Teacher: Is it possible in communication to experience this total energy in the present?

Krishnamurti: You can ask the same question in a different way. You are asking a positive question all the time about something you do not know. Your question is unrelated to the problem. Now how would you put the question?

Teacher: Do you mean to say that the right question should be "When I see the destructive nature of this energy. . . ."

Krishnamurti: See the falseness of this energy which is destructive, that in itself is the answer. You cannot go beyond the destructive nature of this energy and say what the other is.

Can you cease to revolve in creating destructive energy? You will not then ask what the other is. All you can ask is, "Is it possible to stop this self-created destructive energy?" You cannot enquire positively into energy, it must be a negative approach—the comprehending of the fact negatively, not positively, in order to get to the other—because you do not know the other. So your approach must be negative in the sense that you see the factual nature of this energy which is self-destructive.

Can I comprehend negatively? Can I learn a technique, and can the mind liberate itself from the technique without recompense? Then the mind is open to a different pattern of energy.

The entire world is in a vast mess, in confusion. To have a total response to that, you must have energy of a different quality from the usual energy which you apply to a problem. The usual approach to a problem is in terms of hope, fear, success, fulfilment and so on, with its accompanying despair. This is obvious. These are all psychological facts. Here we have a world issue and you have to approach it not with the energy of despair but with an energy which is not contaminated by despair. To come upon that energy which is not destructive, the mind must be free from the energy of despair. This is a world problem, how do you answer it? Do you answer it idealistically with the intention, the desire and the feeling, "This is the right thing to do"? If you do, you answer it with the energy of despair. Or do you look at it with a different energy altogether? If you look at the total problem with that new kind of energy, you will have the right answer.

Teacher: I would like to talk a little more about the communication of this feeling you are hinting at: that we are perpetuating through our education the energy of despair and hence the hopelessness of such education. Can we educate in the accepted sense of the word, and yet have the other? Can a person who is engaged in teaching a certain subject teach that perfectly and yet get the whole, total feeling? Can he do it without a motive, with a total attention to the thing that he is doing and with a feeling of love? Will that help to keep the mind open to the new source of energy?

Krishnamurti: You are introducing suppositions, they are not facts. You see, you have no love. Occasionally there is an opening in the cloud and you see the bright light, but only occasionally. You are not dealing with facts, you are dealing with suppositions. If you were dealing with facts, then you could have answered.

The main statement is not good enough, "I do pay attention sometimes, I do love without wanting something in return." You may do this occasionally, but you have to do it on all the three hundred and sixty five days, not just one day.

Teacher: As I see it, whatever I do, I want to fit the "plus" into this.

Krishnamurti: You cannot put the plus into the minus, you cannot put the creative thing into the destructive. The destructive energy has to cease for the creative thing to come in.

You have time, you have leisure to meditate, and without becoming sentimental you have to discover the destructive energy in yourself. It is a continuous process of awareness, keeping the window open for the other. This is a total process all the time.

There is a psychological climate that is necessary, which means relationship in teaching and that requires subtlety. You cannot have subtlety and pliability if you have an end in mind. If you are thinking from a conclusion, from an experience of knowing a great many techniques, you cannot have pliability, subtlety.

Have you ever talked to anybody who is entrenched deep in some ideal, in some dogma? He has no pliability, no subtlety. To bring about subtlety, pliability, the mind must have no anchorage.

Teacher: Is it possible to arrange circumstances so that this pliability and subtlety come into being? It is not always possible to create this within organisations.

Krishnamurti: How can one create neither antagonism nor resistance in relationship? How is a sense of equality to be brought about? If you can establish that feeling then what is the next step? Is there a next step?

First of all, is it possible to establish mutual confidence

within an organisation? To establish that requires a great deal of intelligence on my part and on the part of others.

Teacher: As you said, the problem is how to establish relationship without the sense of high and low and with the awareness of this total feeling.

Krishnamurti: We do not know anything about this total feeling. But we know the destructive nature of certain forms of energy and the mind tries to disentangle itself from that.

We know there must be equality and that equality is denied when there are divisions, cliques, when we are functioning merely on an economic level and when there is no comprehension of the nature of destructive energy. It is not an economic equality that has to be established but an equality at every level. If we do not establish that right from the beginning and establish it also in ourselves, we have no contact. Can we spend time in considering how to establish an equality in that sense, not the equality of technique? Can we come together to establish between ourselves this feeling of equality in which all differences are gone? Then we are free. We must be quite sure that at least a few of us are walking along the road. Some of us then may walk slowly, some may walk fast but it is in the same direction and the direction is the quality. It is really a turning of one's back to the world. If you see the crippling effects of the energy of despair, you have to renounce it. If you are alive to this, it means that your relationship with the world is entirely different and that opens a great many doors.

10 / On Meditation and Education

Are we human beings or professionals? Our professions take the whole of our lives and we give very little time to the cultivation or the understanding of the mind, which is living. The profession comes first, then living. We approach life from the point of view of the profession, the job, and spend our lives in it and at the end of our lives we turn to meditation, to a contemplative attitude of mind.

Are we only educators or are we human beings who see education as a significant and true way of helping human beings to cultivate the total mind? Living comes before teaching. The man who is a specialist—a nose and throat specialist —spends all his days in the examination of noses and throats and obviously his mind is filled with throats and noses and only occasionally can he think about meditation or look at truth.

Can we go into the question of meditation, as a comprehensive total approach to life which implies the understanding of what meditation is? I do not know if any of you meditate and I do not know what meditation means to you. What part has meditation in education and what do we mean by meditation? We give so much importance to the getting of a degree, the getting of a job, to financial security; that is the entire design of our thinking. And meditation, the real enquiry into whether there is god, the observing, experiencing of that immeasurable state, is not part of our education at all. We will have to find out what we mean by meditation, not how to meditate. That is an immature way of looking at meditation. If one can unravel what is meditation, then the very process of unravelling is meditation.

What is meditation and what is thinking? If we enquire into what meditation is, we have to enquire into what thinking is. Otherwise, merely to meditate when I do not know the process of thinking is to create a fancy, a delusion, which has no reality whatsoever. So to really understand or to discover what meditation is, it is not enough to have mere explanations which are only verbal and therefore have little significance; one has to go into the whole process of thinking.

Thinking is a response of memory. Thoughts become the slave of words, the slave of symbols, of ideas, and the mind is the word and the mind becomes slave to words like god, communist, the principal, the vice-principal, the prime minister, the police inspector, the villager, the cook. See the nuances of these words and the feelings that accompany these words. You say *sannyasi* and immediately there is a certain quality of respect. So the word for most of us has immense significance. For most of us the mind is the word. Within the conditioned, verbal, technical symbolic framework, we live and think; that framework is the past, which is time. If you observe this process taking place in yourself, then it has significance.

Now is there thought without word? Is there thinking without word and therefore out of time? The word is time. And if the mind can separate the word, the symbol, from itself, then is there an enquiry which does not seek an end and is therefore timeless?

First, let us look at the whole picture. A mind that has no space in which to observe has no quality of perception. From thinking, there is no observation. Most of us see through words, and is that seeing? When I see a flower and say it is a rose, do I see the rose or do I see the feeling, the idea that the word invokes? So, can the mind which is of time and space, explore into a non-spatial, timeless state because it is only in that state that there is creation? A technical mind which has acquired specialized knowledge can invent, add to, but it can never create. A mind that has no space, no emptiness from which to see, is obviously a mind that is incapable of living in a spaceless, timeless state. That is what is demanded. So a mind that is merely caught in time and space, in words, in itself, in conclusions, in techniques, in specialization, such a mind is a very distressed mind. When the world is confronted with something totally new, all our old answers, codes, traditions are inadequate.

Now what is thinking? Most of our lives are spent in the effort to be something, to become something, to achieve something. Most of our lives are a series of connected and disconnected constant effort and in these efforts the whole problem of ambition and contradiction brings about a certain exclusive process which we call concentration. And why should we make an effort? What is the point of effort? Would we stagnate if we failed to make an effort and what does it matter if we stagnate? Are we not stagnating with our immense efforts—now? What significance has effort any more? If the mind understands effort will it not release a different kind of energy which does not think in terms of achievement, ambition, and so contradiction? Is not that very energy action itself?

In effort there is involved idea and action and the problem of how to bridge idea and action. All effort implies idea and action and the coming together of these two. And why should there be such division, and is not such a division destructive? All divisions are contradictory and in the self-contradictory state there is inattention. The greater the contradiction the greater the inattention and the greater the resultant action. So life is an endless battle from the moment we are born to the moment we die.

Is it possible to educate both ourselves and students to live? I do not mean to live merely as an intellectual being but as a complete human being, having a good body and a good mind, enjoying nature, seeing the totality, the misery, the love, the sorrow, the beauty of the world.

When we consider what meditation is, I think one of the first things is the quietness of the body. A quietness that is not enforced, sought after. I do not know if you have noticed a tree blowing in the wind and the same tree in the evening when the sun has set? It is quiet. In the same way, can the body be quiet, naturally, normally, healthily? All this implies an enquiring mind which is not seeking a conclusion or starting from a motive. How is a mind to enquire into the unknown, the immeasurable? How is one to enquire into god? That is also part of meditation. How do we help the student to probe into all this? Machines and the electronic brains are taking over, automation is going to come in about fifty years to this country and you will have leisure and you can turn to books for knowledge. Our intelligence, not merely the capacity to reason but rather the capacity to perceive, understand what is true and what is false, is being destroyed by the emphasis on authority, acceptance, imitation, in which is security. All this is going on but in all this what part has meditation? I feel the quality of meditation as I am talking to you. It is meditation. I am talking but the mind that is communing is in a state of meditation.

All this implies an extraordinarily pliable mind, not a mind that accepts, rejects, acquiesces or conforms. So meditation is the unfolding of the mind and through it perception, the seeing without restraint, without a background and so an endless emptiness in which to see. The seeing without the limitation of thought which is time requires a mind that is astonishingly quiet, still.

All this implies an intelligence which is not the result of education, book learning, acquisition of techniques. Obviously, to observe a bird you must be very quiet; otherwise at the least movement on your part the bird flies away; the whole of your body must be quiet, relaxed, sensitive to see. How will you create that feeling? Take that one thing which is part of meditation. How will you bring this about in a school like this? First of all, is it necessary at all to observe, to think, to have a mind that is subtle, a mind that is still, a body that is responsive, sensitive, eager?

We are only concerned with helping the student to get a degree and to get a job and then we allow him to sink into this monstrous society. To help him to be alive it is imperative for a student to have this extraordinary feeling for life, not his life or somebody's else's life, but for life, for the villager, for the tree. That is part of meditation—to be passionate about it, to love—which demands a great sense of humility. This humility is not to be cultivated. Now how will you create the climate for this, because children are not born perfect? You may say that all we have to do is to create the environment and they will grow into marvellous beings; they will not. They are what they are, the result of our past with all our anxieties and fears and we have created the society in which they live and children have to adjust themselves and are conditioned by us. How will you create the climate in which they see all these influences, in which they look at the beauty of this earth, look at the beauty of this valley? Just as you devote time to mathematics, science, music, dance, why do you not give some time to all this?

Teacher: I was thinking about practical difficulties and how it is not always possible.

Krishnamurti: Why do you give time to dance, to music? Why not give time to this as you give to mathematics? You are not interested in it. If you saw that it was also necessary you would devote time to it. If you saw that it was as essential as mathematics, you would do something.

Meditation implies the whole of life, not just the technical, monastic, or scholastic life, but total life and to apprehend and communicate this totality, there must be a certain seeing of it without space and time. A mind must have in itself a sense of the spaceless and the timeless state. It must see the whole of this picture. How will you approach it and help the student to see the whole of life, not in little segments, but life in its totality? I want him to comprehend the enormity of this.

11 / On Flowering

Teacher: I wonder whether we could go into the problem of how to ask the right question? We generally ask a question to find an answer, to arrive at a method, to discover the reason for things. We question to find out why one is jealous, why one is angry. Now, can the quality of questioning be engendered in oneself and in the child so that there is only enquiry without a method or without merely finding reasons? Is not the problem of right questioning of prime importance in our approach to the child?

Krishnamurti: How do we question anything? When do we question ourselves or question authority or question the educational system? What does the word "question" mean? I wonder if a self-critical awareness is lacking in us. Are we aware of what we are doing, thinking, feeling? How do we awaken or question, so as to bring about this critical awareness? If we go into this it might help to arouse in the child a self-critical capacity, a critical awareness. How do we set about it? What makes me question? Do I ever question myself? Do I see how mediocre I am? Or do I question, find an explanation and move on? It is very depressing to discover one's mediocrity and therefore one does not question, and one never goes beyond.

Let us put it differently. Very little of us is alive. A small part of us is throbbing, the rest is asleep. The little part that is throbbing, gradually grows dim, falls into a rut and is finished.

Does one know what it means to be a full human being? The fact is, one is not alive. The question is to be totally alive, to be physically alive, to be in very good health, not to over-eat, to be sensitive emotionally, to feel, to have a quality of sympathy, and to have a very good mind. Otherwise, one is dead.

How would you awaken the mind as a whole? It is your problem. How would you see that you are completely alive inside, and outside; in your feelings, in your taste in everything? And how would you awaken in the student this feeling of non-fragmented living?

There are only two ways of doing it: either there is something within you which is so urgent that it burns away all contradiction; or you have to find an approach which will watch all the time, which will deliberately set about investigating everything you are doing, an awareness which will ceaselessly ask the question to find out in yourself so that a new quality comes into being which keeps all the dirt out. Now, which is it that you are doing as a human being as well as a teacher?

Teacher: Is one to question constantly, or is there a questioning which has its own momentum?

Krishnamurti: If there is no momentum, then you have to start with little things, haven't you? Start with the little things, not the big things. Start observing how you dress, what you say, how you watch the road, without the operation of criticism. And, watching, listening, how are you going to get to the other, which will be the momentum, which carries all by itself?

There is a momentum to which you do not have to pay attention, but you cannot come to it except by watching little things; and yet you have to see that you are not caught in this everlasting watching. To watch one's dress, the sky, and yet be out of it, so that your mind is not only watching little things but absorbing the wider issues, such as the good of the country, and the much wider issues also, such as authority, such as this perpetual desire to fulfil, this constant concern whether one is right or wrong, and fear. So, can the mind observe the little things and without being caught in the little things, can it move out so that it can record much greater issues?

Teacher: What is the state of mind, the approach in which there is this everlasting watching, the understanding of little things, without being caught in the little things?

Krishnamurti: Why are you caught in the little things? What is the thing that makes you a prisoner of the little?

Teacher: My opinions. And yet I do not want to be caught in little things.

Krishnamurti: But I have to pay attention to little things. Most people are caught in them the moment they pay attention. To pay attention and yet not to be prisoner to little things, is the issue. Now, what makes the mind or the brain a prisoner?

Teacher: Concern with the immediate.

Krishnamurti: What do you mean, sir? Do you mean not having a long vision? You are not looking at the problem.

Teacher: My attachment to little things.

Krishnamurti: Are you not a prisoner of little things?

Teacher: I am. With me it is probably a deep unconscious sense, that I am preparing myself for something great, an illusion like that.

Krishnamurti: Are you aware that you are a prisoner of little things? Examine why you are a prisoner. Take the fact that you are a prisoner of little things, and possibly of many little things, ask why, go into it, question it, find out. Do not give an explanation and run off with the explanation which you did just now. You must actually take one thing and look at it. In tackling inwardly the frustration, the conflict, the resistance, you correct the outer. The psychological conflict within expresses itself outwardly in your becoming a prisoner of little things and then you try to correct them. Without understanding the inward conflict, the misery, life has no meaning. If you discover that you are frustrated, then go into it; and if you have gone deeply into it, it will correct the anger, the over-eating, the over-dressing.

The way you question frustration is important. How do you question? So that frustration unfolds, so that frustration flowers? It is only when thought flowers that it can naturally die. Like the flower in a garden, thought must blossom, it must come to fruition and then it dies. Thought must be given freedom to die. In the same way there must be freedom for frustration to flower and die. And the right question is whether can there be freedom for frustration to flower and to die?

Teacher: What do you mean by flowering, sir?

Krishnamurti: Look at the garden, the flowers in front over there! They come to bloom and after a few days they wither away because it is their nature. Now, frustration must be given freedom so that it blossoms. You have to understand the reason of frustration, but not in order to suppress it, not to say, "I must fulfil". Why should I fulfil? If I am a liar I can try to stop lying, which is what people generally do. But can I allow that lie to flower and die? Can I refuse to say it is right or wrong, good or bad? Can I see what is behind the lie? I can only find out spontaneously why I lie if there is freedom to find out. In the same way, in order not to be a prisoner of little things, can I find out why I am a prisoner? I want that fact to flower. I want it to grow and to expand, so that it withers and dies without my touching it. Then I am no longer a prisoner though I watch the little things.

Your question was: "Is there a momentum which keeps moving, keeping itself clean, healthy?" That momentum, that flame which burns, can only be when there is freedom for everything to flower—the ugly, the beautiful, the evil, the good and the stupid—so that there is not a thing suppressed, so that there is not a thing which has not been brought up and examined and burnt out. And I cannot do that if through the little things I do not discover frustration, misery, sorrow, conflict, stupidity, dullness. If I only discover frustration through reasoning I do not know what frustration means. So, from little things I go to something, wider and in understanding the wider, the other things flower without intervention.

Teacher: I seem to catch a glimpse of what you say, I am going to examine it.

Krishnamurti: You are examining it while I am examining it. You are examining your own little things in which you are caught.

Teacher: In the flowering of conflict, there should be freedom to flower and die. The little mind does not give itself that freedom. You are saying that the inward conflict should flower and die and again you said that this flowering and dying is happening as we are examining it now. There is one difficulty, which is, that I seem to project something into this floration and that itself is a hindrance.

Krishnamurti: That is the real crux. You see, to you flowering is an idea. You do not see the fact, the symptom, the cause, and allow that cause to blossom right now. The little mind always deals with symptoms and never with the fact. It does not have the freedom to find out. It is doing the very thing which indicates the little mind, because it says, "It is a good idea, I will think about it," and so it is lost for it is then dealing with ideation, not with fact. It does not say, "Let it flower, and let us see what happens." Then it would discover. But, it says, "It is a good idea; I must investigate the idea".

Now, we have discovered a great many things. First of all,

we are unaware of the little things. Then, becoming aware of them, we are caught in them and we say, "I must do that, I must do this."

Can I see the symptom, go into the cause, and let the cause flower? But I want it to flower in a certain direction, which means I have an opinion on how it should flower. Now can I go after that? That becomes my major issue. And I see that I prevent the cause flowering because I am afraid I do not know what will happen if I allow frustration to flower. So I go after why I am afraid? What am I afraid of? I see, that so long as fear exists there can be no flowering. So I have to tackle fear, not through the idea, but tackle it, as a fact which means I will allow fear to blossom. I will let fear blossom, and see what happens. All this requires a great deal of inward perception.

Allow fear to blossom—do you know what that means? It may mean I may lose my job, be destroyed by my wife, my husband.

Can I allow everything to blossom? It does not mean I am going to murder, rob somebody, but can I just allow "what is" to blossom!

Teacher: Could we go into this, then allowing a thing to blossom?

Krishnamurti: Do you really see the fact? What does it mean, to allow a thing to blossom, to allow jealousy to blossom? First of all, how unrespectable, how unspiritual. How do you allow jealousy to blossom, to achieve a full life? Can you do it so that you are not caught in it? Can you let that feeling have its full vitality, without obstruction? Which means you do not identify yourself with it, which means you do not say it is right or wrong, you do not have an opinion about it; these are all methods of destroying jealousy. But you do not want to destroy jealousy. You want it to blossom, to show all its colours, whatever they may be.

Teacher: It is not very clear to me, sir.

Krishnamurti: Have you grown a plant? How do you do it?

Teacher: Prepare the ground, put in manure. . . .

Krishnamurti: Put in the right manure, use the right seed, put it in at the right time, look after it, prevent things from happening to it. You give it freedom. Why do you not do the same with jealousy?

Teacher: The flowering here is not expressed outside like the plant.

Krishnamurti: It is much more real than the plant you are planting outside in the field. Do you not know what jealousy is? At the moment of jealousy, do you say it is imagination? You are burning with it, are you not? You are angry, furious. Why do you not pursue it, not as an idea but actually, take it out and see that it flowers, so that each flowering is a destruction of itself and therefore, there is no "you" at the end of it who is observing the destruction. In that is real creation.

Teacher: When the flower blossoms, it reveals itself. What exactly do you mean, sir, when you say that when jealousy blossoms it will destroy itself?

Krishnamurti: Take a bud, an actual bud from a bush. If you nip it, it will never flower, it will die quickly. If you let it blossom, then it shows you the colour, the delicacy, the pollen, everything. It shows what it actually is without your being told it is red, it is blue, it has pollen. It is there for you to look at. In the same way, if you allow jealousy to flower, then it shows you everything it actually is— which is envy, attachment. So in allowing jealousy to blossom, it has shown you all its colours and it has revealed to you what is behind jealousy, which you will never discover if you do not allow it to blossom.

To say that jealousy is the cause of attachment is mere verbalisation. But in actually allowing jealousy to flower, the fact that you are attached to something becomes a fact, an emotional fact, not an intellectual, verbal idea and so each flowering reveals that which you have not been able to discover; and as each fact unveils itself, it flowers and you deal with it. You let the fact flower and it opens other doors, till there is no flowering at all of any kind and, therefore, no cause or motive of any kind.

Teacher: Psychological analysis will help me to find out the causes of jealousy. Between analysis and the flowering in which a flower reveals itself, is there a vital difference?

Krishnamurti: One is an intellectual process, the observer operating on the thing observed, which is analysis, which is correction, the altering and the adding. The other is the fact without the observer, it is what the fact is itself.

Teacher: What you say is totally non-verbal. There is no relationship between the observer and the observed.

Krishnamurti: Once you get the feeling that everything in you must blossom, which is a very dangerous state, if you understand this thing, that everything must flower in you, which is a marvellous thing, in that there is real freedom. And, as each thing flowers, there is neither observer nor the observed; therefore there is no contradiction. So all the things blossom in you and die.

Teacher: Why should I allow it to blossom if I can nip it in the bud?

Krishnamurti: What is going to happen to the flower if you kill the bud? If you kill the bud, it will not flower any more. In the same way, you say, "I must kill jealousy or fear" but it is not possible to kill jealousy and fear. You can suppress them, alter them, offer them to some god, but they will always be there. But if you really understand the central fact, to allow everything to flower without interference, it will be a revolution.

Teacher: Jealousy is a complex thing.

Krishnamurti: Let it flower. Jealousy, in flowering, reveals its complexity. And in understanding the complexity, in watching the complexity, it reveals some other factor, and let that blossom, so that everything is blossoming in you, nothing is denied, nothing is suppressed, nothing is controlled. It is a tremendous education, is it not?

Teacher: There is great significance in what you are saying. But is it possible?

Krishnamurti: It is possible, otherwise there is no point in saying it. If you see that, how will you help the student to flower? How will you help him to understand?

Teacher: I would start with myself. By a certain psychological approach I can see the cause. What you are saying is that in flowering, the problem unfolds itself. There is a great deal of difference between the two. But even if I have a glimpse of it, to convey it to the student is difficult.

Krishnamurti: It is a non-verbal communication which I have communicated to you verbally. How have I come to a flowering of thought which takes place in communication?

Teacher: Before one can investigate into this floration or even into the space in which floration can take place, there is a quality of equilibrium which has to be established to allow anything to flower in me.

Krishnamurti: I do not accept it. I do not believe you can do it that way. Take the idea of jealousy. I say make it flower. But you will not let it flower.

Teacher: When I am dealing with a child, is not the first factor this awakening of the quality of perception, which is equilibrium?

Krishnamurti: I will tell you what it is. If you listened, really listened, the flowering would actually take place. If you listened, observed, understood, immediately after the listening, it has taken place if that has taken place, then the other things are very simple to the child. You will find different ways to watch the child, to help the child, to communicate with the child at the verbal level. The very act of listening is the following.

Teacher: Is that listening a quality, sir?

Krishnamurti: You are listening. Why do you call it a quality? You have listened to what I have to say this morning: "Let everything flower."

If you listen, it will take place. It is not a quality. A quality is a thing already established. This is a living thing, a burning thing, a furious thing. You cannot make it a quality, a practice. Can you practice seeing colour? You cannot. You can see the beauty and the glory of the flower only when there is a flowering.